D0083381

*Samuel "Hudibras" Butler*

*Updated Edition*

Twayne's English Authors Series

Bertram H. Davis, Editor

*Florida State University*

TEAS 193

Samuel "Hudibras" Butler (1612/3–1680)

# Samuel "Hudibras" Butler

## Updated Edition

### By George Wasserman

*Russell Sage College*

Twayne Publishers
*A Division of G. K. Hall & Co.* • *Boston*

*Samuel "Hudibras" Butler, Updated Edition*
George Wasserman

Copyright 1989 by G. K. Hall & Co.
All rights reserved.
Published by Twayne Publishers
A Division of G. K. Hall & Co.
70 Lincoln Street
Boston, Massachusetts 02111

Copyediting supervised by Barbara Sutton
Book production by Gabrielle B. McDonald
Book design by Barbara Anderson

Typeset in 11 pt. Garamond
by Huron Valley Graphics of Ann Arbor, Michigan

Printed on permanent/durable acid-free paper
and bound in the United States of America

**Library of Congress Cataloging-in-Publication Data**

Wasserman, George Russell, 1927–
    Samuel "Hudibras" Butler / by George Wasserman. —Updated ed.
        p.  cm.—(Twayne's English authors series ; TEAS 193)
    Bibliography: p.
    Includes index.
    ISBN 0-8057-6973-0 (alk. paper)
    1. Butler, Samuel, 1612–1680—Criticism and interpretation.
I. Title. II. Series.
PR3338.W3  1989
821'.4—dc19                                                88-25906
                                                                CIP

PR
3338
.W3
1989
c.1

ℛℴ

*For Marilyn*

UWEC McIntyre Library

EAU CLAIRE, WI

# Contents

## About the Author

George Wasserman is professor of English at Russell Sage College, Troy, New York. He is the author of *John Dryden* (1964), *Roland Barthes* (1981), *Samuel Butler and the Earl of Rochester: A Reference Guide* (1986), and numerous articles on Restoration literature.

# Preface

There are two reasons for including the name of Samuel Butler's most famous work, *Hudibras,* in the title of this study. First, it is a convenient way to distinguish between our Restoration satirist and the Victorian novelist who is the subject of another volume in this series of critical studies. And second, there is ample precedent for such a designation. Long before the advent of his successor (who was, by the way, no relative), *our* Butler was identified by the name of his poem. Samuel Pepys and other contemporaries frequently referred to him as "Hudibras Butler," or simply as "Hudibras," and the name so appears even in an official court record.

Yet, having said this much, a word of apology is still necessary for the present use of this convention, for to identify Butler with a work that is seldom read any longer (at least in its entirety) is to convey little to the contemporary reader. Indeed, it may have an adverse effect upon him. "Who now reads Butler?" James Sutherland asked in a 1969 volume of the *Oxford History of English Literature:* "In his own day he was enjoyed by readers who were unlikely to read much else, but if he is read at all today it is probably by those who have read so much that they have also read *Hudibras.*" Although Sutherland's words are still generally true today, critical interest in Butler has increased since I first quoted them, largely, I believe, because modern readers are in a better position than earlier readers to understand him. Restoration readers called Butler "Hudibras" because they knew little more of him than this poem. Today, we not only know that poem (and in a text that is superior to those of the Restoration), but also possess Butler's prose Characters, his minor verse, and a voluminous record of his thought and observations, his notebook materials in prose and verse. The updated edition of this study, therefore, continues to emphasize Butler's thought and to interpret *Hudibras* and the Characters as an expression of that thought. Like its predecessor, it attempts to survey all of Butler's writing now in print and, specifically, to show that Butler's satiric vision grows out of his speculations on the unnaturalness of man. Chapter 2—which sets forth Butler's main assumptions about human nature and defines his complex views on reason and art—is therefore basic to the more analytical discussions that follow it. Chapter 3 sketches the satiric action of *Hudibras,* summarizes its background of political and religious controversy, and attempts to define its peculiar form; and Chapter 4, "The Argument and Imagery of *Hudibras,*" treats the poem as a "satire on man." The focus on Butler's views of human nature continues in chapter 5, an examination of Butler's Characters.

The updated edition of this book also attempts to accommodate an important change now taking place in literary studies, one of those shifts in the tacitly agreed-upon ways of reading that periodically occur in the community of academic readers: I refer to the reconstitution of history in literary criticism. The first edition of this study—written in the afterglow of the New Criticism—backed away from the historical aspects of Butler's writing. It attempted to transcend the temporal particularities of *Hudibras* and to locate the value of the poem in general themes that may be said to have permanent relevance. Throughout this revision, I have tried to adjust this imbalance by attending more closely to the Restoration context of Butler's thought and to the traces of living history in his writing.

George Wasserman

*Russell Sage College*

# Acknowledgments

Portions of this book have appeared elsewhere in print in slightly different form. Much of chapter 2 was published as "Samuel Butler and the Problem of Unnatural Man" in *Modern Language Quarterly;* the first four sections of chapter 4 comprised two articles in *Studies in English Literature*, " 'A Strange *Chimaera* of Beasts and Men': The Argument and Imagery of *Hudibras*, Part I" and "*Hudibras* and Male Chauvinism"; and the fifth section of chapter 4 appeared as "Carnival in Hudibras" in *English Literary History*. I wish to thank the editors of these journals for permission to reprint this material here.

# Chronology

1680    Butler's translation, "Cydippe . . . to Acontius" appears
        in *Ovid's Epistles translated by several hands.* Butler dies on
        25 September.

# Chapter One
# Butler's Career

At the end of the short biographical portion of his life of Samuel Butler, Dr. Johnson observed: "In this mist of obscurity passed the life of Butler, a man whose name can only perish with his language. The mode and place of his education are unknown; the events of his life are variously related; and all that can be told with certainty is, that he was poor."[1] Writing in 1779, Johnson had at his disposal three principal sources of information about Butler's life. One was the Oxford antiquarian Anthony à Wood's *Athenae Oxonienses,* a debt that Johnson acknowledged along with Wood's admission of the "uncertainty of his own narrative" even though it was based upon the notes of John Aubrey, who was personally acquainted with Butler. The second source was the brief life that appeared in the 1704 edition of *Hudibras* and was frequently reprinted in later editions; because its author was unknown to him,[2] Johnson considered its authority "disputable." And third, he might have drawn upon the notes of Charles Longueville, the son of the lawyer who, it is said, paid to bury the poet and became his literary executor; Longueville contributed his notes to a biography of Butler by John Lockman, included in the *General Dictionary, translating Bayle* (1734–41).[3] "More than they knew cannot now be learned," Johnson declared of these sources; "nothing remains but to compare and copy them."[4] History appears still to be on the side of Johnson's declaration. The lives that prefaced the numerous nineteenth-century editions of *Hudibras* added nothing to the materials with which Johnson worked, and the modern biographer knows little more than they about Butler the man.[5] But history has also confirmed Johnson's other claim: Butler's name has not perished.

## Life and Works

Samuel Butler was baptized 14 February 1613 (by modern reckoning) at Strensham, a tiny village on the Avon River south of Worcester.[6] His ancestors had been farmers in the area for three generations,

apparently fairly prosperous ones since, in addition to the property at
Strensham leased from the Russell family, local lords of the manor, the
poet's father (also named Samuel) maintained a house and lands in
nearby Barbourne in the parish of Claines.[7] A man of learning, Samuel
senior served as churchwarden at Strensham and as clerk to his land-
lord, Sir John Russell. At his death in 1626, the elder Butler be-
queathed not only a portion of the Barbourne lands to the poet but also
divided a small library among three of his eight children. Samuel, Jr.,
then age fourteen, received, in the terms of his father's will, "all my
Lawe and Latine bookes of Logicke, Rhetoricke, Philosophy, Poesy,
phisicke, my great Dodaneus Herball, and all other my lattine and
greeke bookes whatsoever."[8] Though such a bequest suggests that the
boy showed some promise as a scholar—probably at the King's School
in Worcester[9]—there is no record of his later matriculation at either
Oxford or Cambridge.

Butler's adolescence and early manhood are no more fully documented
than his childhood. He would probably have finished his schooling at
fifteen and gone on to take over the Barbourne farm, to which his name
was still attached in 1628; these lands were surrendered, however, at
some time before 1637.[10] It is generally accepted that during this period
he served as a secretary or attendant to several persons of importance.
Leonard (or, more likely, his son Thomas) Jefferey, magistrate of Earl's
Croome Court, a parish not far from Butler's birthplace, was probably
the first of these employers.[11] Of greater importance for Butler's development was his reputed service to Elizabeth Grey, Countess of Kent, at
whose house in Bedfordshire he would have come into contact with her
legal advisor, the antiquarian and legal historian John Selden (1584–
1654). Butler's contempt for antiquarians (which is hard to reconcile
with his love of the good old English ways) is frequently expressed in his
Characters and notebook observations; but Selden was by no means one of
those "wholly retired from the present."[12] Selden was a collector of
popular ballads, but he was also a benefactor of the newly formed Bod-
leian Library; he was receptive to John Amos Comenius's educational
innovations and to Francis Bacon's reformation of learning; and his circle
of acquaintances included persons of such divergent views as Thomas
Hobbes, Lancelot Andrewes, Ben Jonson, and Michael Drayton, whose
Poly-Olbion he annotated. John Milton spoke of Selden as "the chief of
learned men reputed in this land." To such a man, Butler would not have
been indifferent; and if Selden was not the source of many of the poet's
attitudes—his anticlericalism, his abhorrence of sectaries, his general

advocacy of constitutional monarchy—it is safe to assume that he provided a strong reenforcement of them.[13]

We can only guess that Butler was in his twenties during his employment by the Duchess of Kent; John Aubrey merely says that he came there "when a young man" and that he served her "severall yeares."[14] What Butler was doing during the next twenty years or so is also largely a matter of speculation. He was thirty when Charles raised his standard at Nottingham, thirty-six when the king was executed. Between these two events (22 August 1642 and 30 January 1649), there occurred what Butler and his contemporaries considered the first two civil wars of the Great Rebellion, interspersed in 1647 with those quarrels between Parliament and the army which he turned to comic purpose in *Hudibras*. According to Hardin Craig, whose view is based upon internal evidence in the poem, Butler was writing part 1 of *Hudibras* during these years.[15]

Tradition has filled this gap in Butler's career with a period of service to a Presbyterian member of Parliament, Sir Samuel Luke of Bedfordshire—the man popularly identified as Butler's model for Sir Hudibras. A missing rhyme in Hudibras's speech in the opening canto of the poem—" 'Tis sung, There is a valiant *Mamaluke* / In forrain Land, yclep'd ———— / To whom we have been oft compar'd" (895–97)—suggests that Butler was indeed familiar with Luke's name, though, as Zachary Grey observed, these lines may also be taken as evidence that Hudibras is *not* to be identified with Luke, "it being an uncommon thing to compare a Person with himself."[16] But Ricardo Quintana's discovery in 1933 of two letters—one by Richard Oxenden to his cousin George Oxenden in India, the other by Butler to the same recipient—cast a new light on the circumstances surrounding the composition of *Hudibras*. Richard Oxenden's letter indicates that for some time prior to the publication of part 1 of the poem, Butler lived in London where George Oxenden "did use to meete him in Grasenn [Gray's Inn] Walkes."[17] The poet's letter corroborates this statement by identifying the original of Sir Hudibras as a West Country knight with whom Butler "became Acquainted lodging in y$^e$ same house w$^{th}$ him in Holbourne," a district adjacent to the Inns of Court. Beside providing an authoritative source for the original of Sir Hudibras, Butler's letter supplies the interesting statement that part 1 of *Hudibras* "was written not long before y$^e$ time, when I had first y$^e$ hon$^r$ to be Acquainted w$^{th}$ you [Oxenden]."[18] If Ricardo Quintana is correct in placing Oxenden's meeting with Butler in 1659, there is good reason to believe that the poet was still at work on part 1 at that time.[19]

How long before this date Butler had been living in London is not known. Aubrey noted that "after the king was beaten out of the field" (perhaps in the summer of 1645), the satirist John Cleveland "and Sam. Butler, &c. of Grayes Inne, had a clubb every night."[20] Was Butler, then, a registered member of Gray's Inn, one of the four London law schools and residences of students and their practicing instructors? Aubrey's additional remark that Butler "studied the Common Lawes of England, but did not practice" and T. R. Nash's claim that he had seen Butler's manuscript abridgment of a famous legal work, Coke's *Commentary on Littleton,* suggest that he may have been.[21] Butler's early associations with the family of Leonard Jefferey, an eminent justice of the peace, and with John Selden indicate his movement in that direction, and the Butler-Oxenden correspondence (which also mentions a registered member of Gray's Inn, Edward Kelke, as one of the poet's companions) strengthens the evidence for such a connection. Legal training would be the expected preparation for one who would enter service as a secretary or steward, or who would engage in the sort of political controversy that has been attributed to Butler (much of it addressed to lawyers and adopting, for satiric purposes, their linguistic mannerisms). And his best-known works clearly reveal that he knew no class of men more intimately than the members of the bar—perhaps too intimately to wish to pursue the profession himself. Among the prose Characters, we count no less than seven portraits of legal types (all of them unflattering); and *Hudibras* is filled with legal language—not merely in the speeches of its hero, who is himself a justice of the peace, but in the satiric statements and analogies of its narrator.

Butler's satire of the law is acute and informed. For example, he observes in one of the Characters that "it matters not, whether he [the student at the Inns of Court] keeps his Study, so he has but kept Commons"; in another, he remarks that "*Inns-of-Court* Men intimate their Proficiency in the Law by the Tatters of their Gowns." A metaphorical passage in the Character of "A Lawyer" expresses the intensity of his feelings on the subject: "The Law is like that double-formed ill-begotten Monster, that was kept in an intricate Labyrinth, and fed with Men's Flesh; for it devours all that come within the Mazes of it, and have not a Clue to find the Way out again."[22] Clearly, Butler was more than casually acquainted with the men and matter of English law. Nevertheless, his name is nowhere to be found in *The Register of Admis-*

*sions to Gray's Inn*—nor, for that matter, is that of his drinking companion whom Aubrey also sequestered there, John Cleveland.

Still, Aubrey's early linking of the poet's name with that of another literary figure (and a Royalist satirist at that) is interesting when we consider that portions of part 1 of *Hudibras* may have been taking shape before the 1650s. *Hudibras,* of course, is a rustic poem (in contrast to the more urban flavor of Butler's Characters), and it therefore offers little evidence of the author's familiarity with the city. Occasionally, however, we do find a passage that describes with what seems firsthand detail the town's part in events just preceding the outbreak of actual hostilities. Hudibras's speech to the bear-baiters in part 1, for instance, evokes the enthusiasm of a united party in its resistance to the king's indictment for high treason of Lord Kimbolton and five members of the House of Commons (1642). How different, Hudibras pleads, from this divisive quarrel between a dog and a bear: "Are these the fruits o'th' *Protestation,*" he asks rhetorically,

> Which all the *Saints,* and some since *Martyrs,*
> Wore in their hats, like Wedding-garters,
> When 'twas resolv'd by either House
> *Six Members* quarrel to espouse?
> Did they for this draw down the Rabble,
> With Zeal and Noises formidable;
> And make all *Cries* about the Town
> Joyn throats to cry the *Bishops* down?
> Who having round begirt the Palace,
> (As once a month they do the *Gallows*)
> As Members gave the sign about,
> Set up their throats with hideous shout.
> (1:2, ll. 521–34)

Hudibras describes these shouts as "a strange harmonious inclination / Of all degrees to *Reformation*" (1:2, ll. 553–54), not only because together they constitute a sort of *concordia discors* (and thus ironically attach to a particular political extreme the ideal balance of powers that Royalist apologists sought in the state as a whole), but also because each voice in the chorus abandons its accustomed cry for an improper and unnatural one:

> . . . Tinkers bawl'd aloud, to settle
> *Church-Discipline,* for patching *Kettle.*

> No *Sow-gelder* did blow his horn
> To geld a Cat, but cry'd *Reform*.
> The *Oyster-women* lock'd their fish up,
> And trudg'd away, to cry *No Bishop*.
>                         (1:2, ll. 535–40)

And so on with the cries of *"Mousetrap-men,"* "Botchers," and others. Further comment on the artfulness of these lines is out of place here; I cite them as evidence of Butler's familiarity with the everyday sights and sounds of London and of his ability to recreate the town's reaction to events that occurred in the early 1640s. Such writing is not proof, of course, of firsthand experience; but it is worth noticing that many of the qualities of this passage may also be found in another almost certainly written from experience: that describing the burning of the Rumps (11 February 1660) in part 3 (3:2, ll. 1505 ff.) of *Hudibras*.

Clearly, *Hudibras* was not Butler's first literary effort. His statement in the letter to Oxenden that he knows not how he "fell into y$^e$ way of Scribling w$^{ch}$ I was never Guilty of before nor since"[23] may be taken either as self-effacing modesty or as a reference to the peculiar metrical style of *Hudibras*. Probably by the time Butler met George Oxenden in Gray's Inn walks, he had written at least a few of the many anonymous prose tracts that were later attributed to him—and perhaps some that have not yet been attributed to him. Recently, Hugh de Quehen has given us a skeptical reassessment of Butler's authorship of most of these pieces, but several of them may still be accepted as early productions of Butler's pen. One of these, *The Case of King Charles I. Truly Stated,* is a point-by-point refutation of a scurrilous mock-defense, supposedly written by the king himself—*King Charls His Case* (1649)—written by the regicide John Cook, Master of Gray's Inn and the chief prosecutor at Charles's trial. Butler's *Case* was not published until 1691 when, according to the publisher's preface, *"a new Race of the old Republican Stamp . . . reviv'd the* [forty year old] *Quarrel"* over the prerogatives of the king. The work was then retitled *The Plagiary Exposed.*[24] Also probably by Butler, though not printed until Robert Thyer collected them in the *Genuine Remains* (1759), are "A Speech Made at the Rota" (a club of political theorists organized in 1659 by James Harrington) and "Two Speeches Made in the Rump Parliament, When it was restor'd by the Officers of the Army in the Year 1659," an exchange between " 'an old Member of the House' and 'an Officer of the Army' " that reads like a serious version of the disputes between Hudibras and Ralpho or those between the Presbyterian and Independent statesmen in part 3, canto 2 of *Hudibras*. A fourth work, *Mola Asinaria* (1659), has been accepted as Butler's largely on the authority of Anthony à Wood. The title page ironically attributes it to William Prynne, the Puritan barrister of Lincoln's Inn who, as the type of the compulsive speaker-writer, was a favorite target of Butler's satire. De Quehen is doubtful about Butler's authorship of this work: "there is nothing," he says, "to suggest either that Butler did write it or that he could not have written it" because "its polemic purpose is entirely serious and essentially Prynne's own."[25] On the other hand, the satirist may not have intended to be political, but personal, ridiculing Prynne for his solo verbal effort (the title refers to the biblical "Millstone too heavy for a man to drive") to terminate the extended "Rump" sessions of the Long Parliament. De Quehen more confidently ascribes to Butler the broadside *Lord Roos His Answer to the Marquesse of Dorchester's Letter,* "written the 25 of February 1659[60]". Roos's (John Manners's) ghostwritten *Answer* to his father-in-law Henry Pierpont (Dorchester) commemorates an early episode in what was to become a sensational marital scandal culminating in a divorce and, later, a House of Commons debate on the legality of remarriage which drew the attention of John Milton (a recognized authority on divorce) and the divorce-minded Charles II himself.[26]

Except for occasional glimpses of the parodic talent that was to follow—the "Speech Made at the Rota," for instance, is a pedantic reduction of the word "Rump" to its literal, or *"fundamental,"* sense—or as early examples of Butler's skill in satiric impersonation, these works have little other value than their suggestion that Butler may have found employment as a royalist pamphleteer during the years of the Common-wealth.[27] More interesting to the general reader may be two anonymous ballads, included by Thyer in the *Genuine Remains.* One, "Upon the Parliament which Deliberated about Making Oliver King" (written probably about the time of the event it celebrates, February 1657), exploits the comic incongruities implicit in the Protector's appointees to his House of Lords and in the regal pretensions of his family:

> Yet old Queen Madge,
> Though things do not Fadge,
>     Wil serve to be Queen of a May-pole;
> Two Princes of Wales,

>         For Whitsun-Ales,
>             And her Grace Mayd-Marrian Claypool.
>                                     (*Satires,* 107)

The other, a quite cryptic riddle entitled simply "A Ballad," begins "A stranger Thing / Then this I sing / Came never to this City," and ends with the wish that

>         God save the king, and Parlament,
>             And eke the Princes highness;
>                 And quickly send
>                 The wars an end. . . .
>                                     (*Satires,* 112)

Predating the execution of Charles I, "A Ballad" may be Butler's earliest verifiable poem; and the reference to "Fleetstreet," where this strange monster may "now" be viewed, appears to place him in London at some time before the end of January 1649.

Though it appears that Butler for several years before the Restoration had been randomly writing the bits and pieces of what was to become the poem *Hudibras,*[28] the "First Part" of that work was not yet ready for the press when Charles entered London on 29 May 1660. In fact, it was not listed in the *Stationer's Register* until 11 November 1662. It is possible that Butler was putting the finishing touches to the work in Shropshire, where, between January 1661 and January 1662, we know he served as steward of Ludlow Castle, the property of Richard Vaughn, Earl of Carbery and, since the Restoration, Lord President of Wales;[29] and the remark in his letter to Oxenden (19 March 1663), that he "was Absent from the Towne" when the book was printed, suggests that he may have stayed on there, perhaps as Vaughn's secretary, until the end of 1662. Wilders hints that Carbery may have been an important contact for Butler, possibly the connection by which he was presented to Charles II and, in September 1667, the poet's protector against arrest for some unknown reason.[30] In any case, the "First Part" of the poem, though dated 1663, was on sale in December of 1662, and "Hudibras," if not the anonymous author, quickly became a household word. As Richard Oxenden's letter to his brother indicates, however, Butler's authorship became common knowledge within a few months—indeed, before long, the author would be known not as Samuel, but as Hudibras Butler. The poet himself, in his letter to Oxenden, attested to the general esteem accorded *Hudibras*—"especially by y$^e$ King & y$^e$ best of his Subjects"—as did even Samuel Pepys, who personally disliked the poem and who sold his copy (at a loss) on 26 December, only to buy another two months later, conceding that it was "certainly some ill humor to be so against that which all the world cries up to be the example of wit."[31] By the end of 1663 nine editions of *Hudibras* had appeared, four of them pirated.[32]

As the title page of the "First Part" indicates, Butler had from the beginning conceived of a second part of the satire and probably during 1662 made some progress on it. Clearly Hudibras's wish, at the end of part 1, that he and Ralpho "stop here, / And rest our weary'd bones awhile" implies a sequel; and a reference earlier in canto 3 (ll. 309 ff.) to the knight's romantic interest in a widow was surely made with a view to the central episode of Hudibras's courtship in the "Second Part." But it seems unlikely that Butler had finished more than a rough sketch of the sequel at this time or, as John Wilders has suggested,[33] that his publisher was waiting to gauge the success of the "First Part" before venturing upon the publication of a second. Since the success of part 1 was immediate, Butler would naturally have wanted to capitalize on it. A prompt sequel might also have prevented the appearance of a spurious second part by an unknown author in May or June 1663, a satire on "Sir William B———ton," probably the parliamentary leader Brereton. When Butler's own "Second Part" at last appeared—again anonymously—at the end of 1663 (but again bearing the publication date of the following year), Butler followed Cervantes's example in making satiric capital of this bogus sequel by working its details into the astrologer Sidrophel's horoscope of the hero in the final canto of his own sequel:

> . . . This *Scheme* of th'Heavens set
> Discovers how in fight you met
> At *Kingston* with a *May-pole Idol,*
> And that y' were bang'd both back and side wel
> And though you overcame the *Bear,*
> The *Dogs* beat You at *Brentford Fair*
> (2:3, ll. 991–96)

and then by permitting his own hero to deny their authenticity:

> . . . I now perceive,
> You are no *Conj'rer,* by your leave,

That *Paultry story* is untrue,
And forg'd to cheat such *Gulls* as you.
(2:3, ll. 999–1002)

The four or more editions of the spurious second part of *Hudibras*[34] and the two editions of Butler's authentic sequel confirm the report on 10 December by Pepys, who still could not "see enough where the wit lies," that *Hudibras* was "now in greatest fashion for drollery."

The extent to which Butler profited from the success of *Hudibras* is difficult to determine. John Aubrey remarked that the king and Lord Chancellor Hyde "both promised him great matters, but to this day he haz got *no* employment,"[35] gossip that would become common knowledge and make Butler the favorite example for writers (for example, Dryden, Otway, and Oldham) addressing the theme of royal ingratitude. Indeed, in spite of the court's evident delight in the poem, the only indication before 1677 of any monetary reward from the king is an item of 30 November 1674, in the *Calendar of Treasury Books,* that records the granting to Butler of two-hundred pounds.[36] Still, even after his loss of profits through piracies of the "First Part," Butler's share of the sales of *Hudibras* must have been considerable, as Anthony à Wood suggested,[37] and such an inference may be strengthened by the absence of any evidence of Butler's employment until about 1669 or 1670, when he appears to have entered a term of service to George Villiers, Duke of Buckingham. Perhaps we should not attach too much significance to what is merely another gap in the records of Butler's career. It is possible, as his early biographers suggested, that a fortunate marriage purchased a brief retirement from the public scene. We know that Butler married; he began an undated letter to his sister thus: "I have read your letter, that you sent my wife . . ."—but whether or not this was the "good jointuresse" on whom Aubrey said he lived "comfortably" cannot be determined.[38]

What evidence we have of Butler's literary activity after the publication of part 2 of *Hudibras* suggests a leisure spent not only in reading and observation (probably the established regimen of his life), but in what must also have been his own intellectual amusement—in the composition, for example, of the prose Characters, many of which, according to Robert Thyer, the possessor of the original manuscripts, were dated by the author in the years 1667 to 1669.[39] Butler was probably also recording his notebook observations about this time; Hugh de Quehen finds no datable evidence in them earlier than October 1665 or later than 1677.[40] De Quehen's further remark that from 1668 until 1674 Butler concentrated on verse[41] permits us to place in these years, then, the composition of a number of specifically Restoration verse satires that focus upon the aberrations of court life and the absurdities of contemporary literature and learning. The mock "Panegyric upon Sir John Denham's Recovery from his Madness"—an event that occurred late in 1669—is typical of these poems. Here, Butler equates Denham's "madness" with the early acts of fraud and theft on which his fortune was reputed to rest and describes his treatment by the doctors as the loss of that fortune. He concludes, however, that "some have guest, / Your *After-wit* is like to be your best" since "nothing, but your Brain, was ever found / to suffer Sequestration, and Compound" (*Satires*, ll. 13–14, 69–70), implying a parallel between the old knight's "recovery" and the "sanity" of a restored England. Nevertheless, two other satires written about 1669 hint at Butler's association with the profligate and often brilliant wits who both animated and scandalized the court of Charles II. One of these, a mock encomium "To the Honourable Edward Howard," was printed in the third part of Jacob Tonson's *Miscellany Poems, Examen Poeticum* (1693), where it was misascribed to Edmund Waller. According to John Harold Wilson, this was Butler's entry in a "wit contest" held at Buckingham's London residence to ridicule Howard's infamous heroic poem, "The British Princes."[42] Howard's response to this fusillade of abuse prompted Butler's doubly damaging mock "Palinodie" or apology for his earlier criticism. Among other ambiguous compliments to the unfortunate author, Butler remarks in the apology that "when the paper's charged with your rich wit, / 'Tis for all purposes and uses fit," noticing in particular that it

> Has an abstersive virtue to make clean
> Whatever Nature made in man obscene.
>
> . . . . . . . . . . . . . .
>
> Cooks keep their pies from burning with your wit,
> Their pigs and geese from scorching on the spit.
> (*Satires*, ll. 85–96)

One wonders whether John Dryden (Howard's brother-in-law) had these lines in mind when, in *Mac Flecknoe*, he spoke of the pages of Thomas Shadwell as "Martyrs of Pies and Reliques of the Bum." Butler's name was first linked with Buckingham's by Anthony à

Wood, who claimed that Butler, along with Thomas Sprat, Martin Clifford, and perhaps others, assisted the duke in the writing of *The Rehearsal,* a theatrical burlesque of heroic drama that was begun before the theaters were closed by the plague in 1665 (4: 209). This is rather early for Butler to be moving in the duke's circle, and Hugh de Quehen completely denies Butler's contribution to the play on the grounds that it "contains nothing recognizable as his" ("An Account," 263). Such a criterion would deny as well, however, the assistance of Clifford and Sprat, which is unquestioned. Although it is impossible to prove that Butler had a hand in either the original writing of the play or its revision for the first performance at the end of 1671, it does not seem necessary to reject Wood's claim. Certainly, after the initial success of *Hudibras* in 1663, Buckingham would have regarded Butler as the preeminent writer of burlesque in the land, and by 1670 or earlier Butler had become formally attached to the duke as a secretary. For his own part, Butler's satiric interest in heroic drama is evident in his comic "Repartees between Cat and Puss at a Caterwauling," which was probably composed during these years of the greatest popularity of this dramatic mode.

With the fall from power of the Earl of Clarendon, the king's chief minister, in 1667, Buckingham became the most powerful member of Charles's Privy-Council, a group that came to be known as the Cabal, from the first initials of each of its members' names and, by chance, for its similarity to the Hebrew word *Kabala* with its connotation of secrecy. When, in the summer of 1670, he was sent to France to negotiate the terms of what has come to be known as the *"Traité Simulé"* (that is, the bogus treaty devised by Charles to conceal his illegal concessions to Louis XIV in the secret Treaty of Dover), Buckingham was accompanied by Butler, Sprat, and Clifford. We can only guess what their duties were, but it is worth noticing that in his prose Character of "An Embassador," Butler remarked that "the greatest Part of his Qualification consists in the Bravery of his Followers, and he carries his Abilities on his Servant's Backs" (178). When the company returned at the end of the summer, it brought along not only the draft of the new treaty, but a new mistress for Charles, Louise de Kéroualle, "The Damned, Dirty Duchess [of Portsmouth]," as one of her many lampooners would later label her. Butler, of course, would have had no part in acquiring either property, but Hugh de Quehen cites a passage from the prose observations that probably reflects his understanding of the implicit danger of the political mission: "The Interests of the King and his

Parliament (though they are really the Same) yet by Factions are rendered so different; that hee is constrained in Reason rather to trust to a Treaty with his most Implacable Enemyes: then Venture a Conference with his great Councell" (xxvii).

Butler was no Francophile. His notebook observations include a section of largely derogatory judgments of Paris, its people, and its language, though he seems not to have had himself much more than a tourist's knowledge of the latter, since the notebook also contains a self-compiled English-French dictionary.[43] It was perhaps the seasoned traveler's impatience with his countrymen's craze for French manners and style that prompted him on his return to write a "Satire" ("upon our ridiculous' imitation of the French," to use Thyer's expanded title) and a Pindaric ode *To the Memory of the most renowned Du-vall*, the last published in 1671, the only verse satire except *Hudibras* to be published in his lifetime. Claude Duval was a famous highwayman, French by birth, though known for his exploits in England, where he was hanged in 1670. Butler's mock encomium of the "hero" is also a general satire of misplaced values, exposing the absurdity of certain literary postures (the Pindaric ode, heroic tragedy, and romance) and of mystical learning (the highwayman practices the "Hermetick Arts" of finding hidden treasure); it attacks the dishonesty of lawyers (whom Duval permitted to practice in their "own allow'd High-way"), and ridicules the sympathies of women who "strove who should have the honour to lay down / And change a life with him." In short, Duval taught a "dull English Nation" how "to hang in a more graceful fashion."

Butler's French experience may have had one more literary consequence, the translation of Nicolas Boileau's second satire, "*La Rime et la Raison*," a witty choice by the poet whose own rhyming practice resolved the technical problem addressed by Boileau—the distortion of meaning for the sake of rhyme—by exploiting the discrepancies of sound and sense in rhyme. Butler's "Satyr on Rhyme" (to use Lamar's title for the translation) is especially interesting for its early attention to Boileau, an important influence on English neoclassicism, particularly as a model for the developing literary mode known as "imitation," a translation that accommodates names and topics contemporary with the translator. According to Harold Brooks, Restoration imitations drew upon two models: one exemplified by Boileau's very free translations of the Roman satirists, the earliest English reference to which he finds in 1673; the other, a native English tradition, in which contemporary interpolations occur within an otherwise faithful translation, is exemplified by Abraham Cowley and, interestingly, by Butler's colleague, Thomas Sprat.[44] Butler's translation of Boileau works within the English tradition of imitation, interpolating only one local detail into its French original—though even this has been given a peculiarly Butleresque twist; in translating the couplet "*Si je pense exprimer un auteur sans defaut, / La raison dit Virgile, et la rime Quinault,*" Butler replaced the French name with an English one—or, rather, contrived a rhyme that forces the reader to supply one—"Ned Howard": "When I would praise an Author, the untoward / Damn'd Sense, says *Virgil,* but the Rhime————" (*Satires,* ll. 21–22). Butler's translation may not be dated with any certainty, however. Its implied reference to Howard places it, no doubt, after the appearance of the *British Princes* (1669)—early indeed; it seems more likely, though, that Butler worked on the translation while in France, and perhaps in the interested presence of Thomas Sprat, in the summer of 1670.

Sprat was Buckingham's chaplain during Butler's tenure as secretary to the duke; he was also an enthusiastic member of the Royal Society and the author of its first history, published in 1667. Butler's references to Sprat's *History* in the prose observations written in the late 1660s tell us little about his views on science—unless we take as implicit criticism his use of the book as a compilation of curious opinions or as a companion volume of Pliny's *Natural History*. Nevertheless, Sprat probably had to count Butler among those "terrible men" whose "power," he wrote near the end of the *History,* he dreaded—the "Wits and Railleurs of this Age": "I confess I believe that *New Philosophy* need not (as *Ceasar*) fear the pale, or the melancholy, as much as the humourous, and the merry: For they perhaps, by making it ridiculous, becaus they themselves are unwilling to take pains about it, may do it more injury than all the Arguments of our severe and frowning and dogmatical *Adversaries.*"[45] Butler's lack of sympathy with such a sentiment may be gauged by the fact that in part 2 of *Hudibras,* written probably in 1663, his charlatan astrologer-scientist Sidrophel also complained of "those whole-sale *Criticks,* that in *Coffee- / Houses,* cry down all *Philosophy* (2:3, ll. 809–10). But Sprat could also have been thinking of works like Butler's "Occasional Reflection on Dr. Charlton's Feeling a Dog's Pulse at Gresham-College" or of the octosyllabic version of "The Elephant in the Moon," an early manuscript draft of which he might have heard of if not read.[46]

Butler appears to have remained in Buckingham's service through 1674. Probably, he attended the duke on a diplomatic visit to The

Hague to negotiate a peace treaty with the Dutch in 1672 and, in the
following year, served him yet in his office of chancellor of Cambridge
University.[47] Thereafter, there is no evidence of any further connection
between Butler and Buckingham. It is unlikely that this reflects much
more than Buckingham's straitened circumstances following his social
disgrace and fall from power in 1674. Certainly, Butler could not have
been shocked by any new revelation of the duke's character; he had
expressed his view of that (". . . one that has studied the whole Body of
Vice . . .") at least five years earlier in a prose Character called "A
Duke of Bucks" (66). Nor would Buckingham's alliance in 1675 with
the parliamentary opposition have made much difference to Butler,
who remarked early in his prose observations that while "there is nothing in Nature more Arbitrary than a Parliament . . . there is nothing
Else that is able to preserve the Nation from being Govern'd by an
Arbitrary Power . . ." (4). Butler's support of monarchy was instinctive, but he was not blind to its faults, and he condemned folly and
ignorance wherever he found them. Thus, while he was revising *Hudibras* for a combined and annotated edition of parts 1 and 2 which was to
appear in 1674, he may also have been at work on a "Satyr on the
Licentious Age of Charles the 2d., Contrasted with the Puritanical One
that Preceded It," in which he observed that

> . . . Men, who one Extravagance would shun,
> Into the contrary Extreme have run;
> And all the Difference is, that as the first
> Provokes the other Freak to prove the worst;
> So, in return, that strives to render less
> The last Delusion, with its own Excess.
> (ll. 27–32)

The new edition of *Hudibras* was the first to include the knight's
"Epistle to Sidrophel," the interregnum astrologer in part 2 who in the
"Epistle" takes on the features of Sir Paul Neile, an amateur astronomer
and one of the founders of the Royal Society. Perhaps, too, a second,
pentameter (or "long verse") version of "The Elephant in the Moon" and
the fragmentary "Satyr upon the Royal Society" were composed by this
time, for the former work contains an allusion to Henry Stubbe's
celebrated attack upon the Society in 1670–71.[48]
     In the summer of 1677, the appearance of Thomas Rymer's *Tragedies
of the last Age Consider'd and Examin'd by the Practice of the Ancients*

probably prompted Butler's defense of the classic English theater in a
verse satire "Upon Critics Who Judge of Modern Plays Precisely by the
Rules of the Ancients." (A serious response to Rymer's critical attack
appears as one of the longest passages of the prose observations [184–
87].) In this year, too, he received word of Charles's long promised
and, finally, rather disappointing favor. Perhaps the announcement of a
third and final part of *Hudibras,* registered on 22 August, reminded the
king of his neglect of the poet; for Butler obtained on 10 September a
royal injunction giving him the sole rights to the publication of any
and all parts of the poem,[49] thus protecting him against the piracies
that had earlier diminished his profits from the success of the first two
parts. The "Third Part" was on sale early in November and went
through five editions—three of them dated 1678.[50] (Butler took note
of his publishers' habit of postdating the various parts of *Hudibras* in his
Character of "A Stationer," one who "begins and ends the year, like a
*Jew,* at pleasure, which is commonly in November, after which all he
prints bears date the year following" [315].) In the same month, Butler
was at last granted a gift of one hundred pounds, together with an
annual pension of an equal amount; apparently, however, the pension
was not paid until September of the following year, when the king
issued instructions that the annuity be paid quarterly and that the
arrears also be honored.[51]

   In view of these gifts, it is somewhat difficult to credit fully the
stories of Butler's poverty in his last years. It is possible that Butler—
who might well have expected greater things from the king, and who
sadly observed in one of his verse fragments that "Great wits have only
been Preferd / In Princes Traines to be interd"—encouraged this image
of himself. It is also possible that Charles—whose tardiness in paying
Dryden, his laureate and historiographer, is well known—failed to
fulfill his good intentions toward the poet and that the additional
twenty pounds "of free guift and royal bounty"[52] granted Butler in
1680 may have been offered in compensation or as an earnest of good
faith. Nevertheless, Butler's poverty seems to have been real. In his last
years, he lived in Rose Alley, Covent Garden, a rather poor neighbor-
hood, described in a parish report as "fitt for mechanicks only and
persons of meane quallitie."[53] Aubrey reported that Butler was confined
with gout to a room there from October 1679 until 1680 (1: 136). It
would have been during this time of confinement that Butler wrote
what was probably his last published poem, a translation of Ovid's
"Cydippe, Her Answer to Acontius," quite an unexpected production

from the author of the mock-heroic epistles of *Hudibras*. Perhaps the enterprising publisher Jacob Tonson counted on this novelty when he commissioned Butler to translate the poem for a collection of *Ovid's Epistles Translated by Several Hands*. For *Hudibras* was not yet forgotten. In 1678, two more editions of the combined first and second parts of the poem appeared. Whiggish efforts to keep alive the fears and suspicions generated by the Popish Plot produced a Tory reaction that fostered the belief that "1641 was come again," and in 1679 and 1680 two more issues of the "Third Part" of *Hudibras* appeared. (There would be no combined edition of all three parts until 1684.) In the final months of his life, Butler was probably reflecting on the views of the exclusion crisis and apparently recognized in the situation a new market for an unpublished work he had written thirty years earlier.[54] *The Case of King Charles I* was not published until 1691, however, for on 25 September 1680, at the age of sixty-seven, Butler died, and two days later was buried in the churchyard of St. Paul's, Covent Garden. His grave and its commemorative plaque are no longer to be found; but a bust of the poet, directly above that of Edmund Spenser and flanked by those of Jonson and Milton, is the cynosure of the Poet's Corner in Westminster Abbey.

## *The Genuine Remains* and Manuscripts

It is generally accepted that the costs of Butler's funeral were borne by William Longueville, an eminent lawyer who supported the poet in his later years and who acquired his papers at his death. After passing through several hands, these manuscripts came at last to Robert Thyer, keeper of the public library in Manchester, who in 1759 published portions of them in two volumes entitled *The Genuine Remains in Verse and Prose of Mr. Samuel Butler*. Earlier, in 1715 and 1717, three volumes entitled *The Posthumous Works in Prose and Verse of Mr. Samuel Butler* had appeared. These can only be considered as a bookseller's attempt to capitalize upon Butler's enduring fame. Of the numerous works attributed to Butler in these volumes, only four are accepted as his by both Lamar and de Quehen: the ode *To . . . Du-Vall*, *The Case of King Charles I*, *Two Letters, One from John Audland . . . The Other, William Prynne's Answer*, and *Mola Asinaria*, although de Quehen has some doubt about the last of these. A fifth work, *Mercurius Menippeus*, published in 1682 and included in the *Posthumous Works* as "Memoirs of the Years 1649 and 50," is reprinted by Lamar, but de Quehen more convincingly ascribes it to Thomas Winyard ("An Account," 274). The contents of *The Genuine Remains,* based almost entirely on Butler's manuscript material, may be taken as genuine Butler, however. Thyer's first volume includes 121 of the poet's prose Characters—never printed in the author's life—and selections from his classified prose observations. His second volume includes all but two (*Mola Asinaria* and *Lord Roos His Answer*) of the minor works mentioned in the present chapter, a "Poetical Thesarus" of tentative lines on various subjects, and a number of more or less finished poems.

The latter may be cited here under two general headings: first, several formal satires, "Upon the Weakness and Misery of Man," "Upon Gaming," "Upon Drunkenness," "Upon Marriage," "Upon Plagiaries," and "Upon the Imperfection and Abuse of Human Learning" (the last in two parts, the second being unfinished); and second, a collection of miscellaneous pieces that includes a prologue and epilogue to William Habbington's old play, *The Queen of Arragon,* revived in 1668 as a birthday celebration for the Duke of York. Although only a few of these poems are written in the rough octosyllabic couplets we have come to identify with Butler and although several of the formal satires want his characteristic sense of the ludicrous, all of these pieces are unquestionably his. The subjects of several of them Butler treated in his prose Characters, and restatements of many of their ideas and turns of phrase occur again and again in *Hudibras* and in the manuscript notebook materials in prose and verse.

In 1885, the bulk of Butler's surviving manuscript material ("no more than half the total left" by the poet [*Prose Observations,* xxi]) was acquired by the British Museum. This material consists of two folio volumes, one in Butler's hand (Add. MSS. 32625), the other (Add. MSS. 32626) a transcription by Robert Thyer of no longer extant holograph, portions of which he published in The *Genuine Remains.* A third manuscript volume, once believed also to be in Butler's hand, disappeared from scholarly attention until 1941, when Dr. A. S. W. Rosenbach listed it in his catalog of *English Poetry to 1700.* Hugh de Quehen in 1972 identified this manuscript as William Longueville's transcription of selected passages from the original manuscripts he received at Butler's death.[55] The extent of the manuscript material is considerable: according to de Quehen, the British Museum MS. (32625) contains "15,700 lines of miscellaneous verse and a thousand passages of miscellaneous prose averaging about ninety words per passage"; to this must be added the unique passages in Thyer's and

Longueville's transcriptions, the latter alone preserving 180 passages from manuscripts now lost.[56]

The manuscript material considered in the next chapter was arranged by Butler under thirteen general headings: "Learning and Knowledge," "Truth and Falshood," "Religion," "Wit and Folly," "Ignorance," "Reason," "Virtue and Vice," "Opinion," "Nature," "History," "Physique," "Princes and Government," and "Criticisms upon Books and Authors." (Thyer grouped additional passages under the heading "Sundry Thoughts.") It is unlikely that this collection of material—some of it like Baconian aphorisms, some of it like short essays—was ever intended by Butler for publication. More probably, it served as a convenient means of keeping at hand witty or thoughtful elaborations of personal insights and reflection for inclusion in other works. Dr. Johnson suggested this when he described the materials in Thyer's possession as *"Hudibras* in prose," a repository of "thoughts that were generated in his own mind which might be usefully applied to some future purpose."[57] For example, under the heading "Religion" in the notebook, Butler noted the following: "Because the Scripture says obedience is better then Sacrifice, Sectarys believe the less of it wil serve" (*Prose Observations,* 26). Butler used this observation in his Character of "An Hypocritical Nonconformist"—"And because the Scripture says, *Obedience is better than Sacrifice,* he believes the less of it will serve" (48)—and again in the Character of "An Anabaptist"—"He believes, because Obedience is better than Sacrifice, the less of it will serve" (217). Another example may be found just below the passage on sectarian obedience in Butler's manuscript: "Presbyterians," Butler wrote there, "cry down the Common Prayer because there is no Ostentation of Gifts in it, with which the People are most taken, and therefore they esteeme it but as lost time" (26). Again we find among the Characters that the "Hypocritical Nonconformist" "cries down the Common-Prayer, because there is no Ostentation of Gifts to be used in the reading of it, without which he esteems it no better than mere loss of Time, and Labour in Vaine, that brings him in no Return of Interest . . ." (49). Such passages in the prose Characters (and there are dozens of other examples) may represent a third stage in the refinement of Butler's observations. The final folios placed in the British Museum consist of a collection of unclassified notes in rather rougher form than the classified notes that precede them. These appear to be Butler's original jottings which, Hugh de Quehen maintains, he gradually "transferred with minor alterations to the classified groups"[58] and then introduced into specific works.

Butler seems to have followed a similar procedure in the composition of verse, although the unstated editorial practices of René Lamar[59]— the editor of the Cambridge edition of Butler's minor verse—make illustration somewhat uncertain. One example may be cited, however. The prose passage on the Puritan use of the Book of Common Prayer appears twice among the passages of miscellaneous verse, once under "Religion" in the "Poetical Thesaurus":

> [The Saints] Abhord to Read the Common-Prair, as vaine,
> And Superstitious, Popish, and Profane:
> But Really, because th' have no Occasions,
> By Spelling, to Hold-forth their Dispensations:
> And th' Ablest of their Brethren, have no shifts,
> For Setting off the Meanest, of their Gifts
>
> *(Satires,* 278–79)

and again, under the same heading in the section labeled "Tentative Lines on Various Subjects":

> [They] Despise the Common-Prayer, as vaine
> And Superstitius, and Profane,
> Because they meet with no Occasions
> To shew by reading Dispensations,
> And ablest Saint[s] can make no shifts
> To hold forth, the meanest of their gifts
>
> *(Satires,* 446)

Lamar's policy of rearranging passages also conceals the presence of at least one embryonic poem in the manuscript material. When Josephine Bauer discovered 252 lines of a narrative satire on medicine[60] in several numbers of the *London Magazine* for 1825–26, she relocated all but a few of the lines under the heading "Physique" in the "Thesaurus" and appendix of Lamar's edition. The story, we might notice in passing, concerns a doctor, who had discovered a "Universal Cure, for all Diseases," and his wife, who was given as her household allowance only those fees her husband received for curing patients of one "slight Disease." *"She must have more Diseases of her own,"* she complains to her husband, who angrily observes that the perversity of women is the one disease his panacea cannot cure. The wife reminds her doctor-husband of his indebtedness to the "Little Beggerly Infirmities" of her sex, for his earliest success came about through his treatment of veneral diseases. Forced to concede the truth of this statement, the doctor must change his defense: the operating costs of quackery are high; the wife will therefore have to employ thrift in the management of her household affairs. Here the sequence ends, but whether Butler left the poem unfinished or continued it in verses not recognized as belonging to it has not yet been determined. Our answer to this and many other questions concerning Butler's working methods must await the publication of a complete edition of Butler's verse.

## Chapter Two

# Butler's Thought

For Butler and his age, the terms "nature" and, with certain empiricist qualifications, "reason" expressed the traditional optimistic sanctions of both intelligibility in the universe and intelligence in man. Butler believed that "the Original of Reason proceede's from the Divine wisdome"; that "the Order of Nature is but a Copie which the Divine wisdome has drawn of it self, and committed to the Custody of Nature"; and that man alone, thanks to his rational endowment, "has the Honor, and Priviledge" to read "this Booke of Nature . . . which lead's him immediatly to God" (66:1).[1] Human reason Butler defined as the faculty by which the mind "put's the Notions, and Images of things . . . that are confused in the understanding, into the same order and condition, in which they are really disposed by Nature, or event," *truth* being the "Right Performance" of this operation (65:1). Thus, in nature's order and in man's awareness of his own place within this order, lies all the knowledge needed in this world.

But theoretical regularity did not blind Butler to the real ambiguities in men. Though nature's variations are all conformable to general law, "the variations of human Reason" are not (65:2). The very fact that truth "has no variations to be allowd for, nor alterations from its own originall Simplicity," seemed to him to make it not inviolable but only more susceptible to undermining falsehood, which "has change of faces and every one proof against all impression" (24:3). Butler assayed "the Generall Temper of mankind" as "a Mixture of Cheat and Folly"; and reason—far from leading man to truth—often merely exchanges the real world for "another kinde of Fooles Paradise of what should be, not what is" (11:2). Indeed, Butler's observations about men appear to contradict the rational harmony of man and nature that is implicit in the philosophical assumptions of his era. Ricardo Quintana has suggested that Butler avoided coming to grips with this contradiction: Butler "never genuinely asked," he writes, "why it should be that truth is attainable only through the cautious and rigorous exercise of reason, and that in consequence the world lies subject to all the 'variations of reason' brought in by the fools and knaves." Quintana argues that Butler's belief in a rational order throughout nature prevented him from naturalizing human defects; therefore, the human tendency to violate that order could be regarded by him only as "essentially unnatural."[2] Although Butler did fail to resolve this paradox, it must also be said that he was very much aware of it. Indeed, his conviction that man is unnatural but *not irrational* is one of the central tenets of his theory of human nature.

## Reason

Butler himself has suggested an approach to the paradox of man's unnaturalness in his peculiar interpretation of the myth of the Fall of Man—specifically, in his assertion that "man was not created Rationall" (194:6); that Adam's innocence (the capacity to believe without understanding) was tantamount to what, in the world of the fallen, would be termed ignorance (62; 15:4); and that reason, purchased through the Fall, was to become not only the means of man's redemption, but also—and most importantly—the means of his punishment. Contrary to many seventeenth-century thinkers who interpreted the loss of paradise as a forfeiture or an impairment of superior intellectual powers, Butler apparently felt that Adam lost only the "priviledges" of ease and innocence with Eden. The Restoration philosopher Joseph Glanvill, for instance, believed that "the human understanding and senses suffered a simultaneous jar at the Fall which threw them out of the perfect prelapsarian focus which made Adam the envy of the angels."[3] Animals, he believed, "are probably less inferior to us in wisdom than we are to Adam."[4] For Butler, however, the innocent Adam understood little more than the animals; for "Providence" supplied for all creatures before the Fall what they lacked in mind (56:2; 58:3).

The Fall itself, Butler believed, was an error that demonstrated the absence of Adam's sense and judgment; "for if his eies had been open before he tasted the Forbidden Fruite, He would never have forfeited the whole Orchard of Paradise for one Apple of it" (15:3). By believing Satan's promise that he could know what God knows—by ignoring, that is, the differences between man and God—Adam accepted for truth what Butler and his century would call "opinion" (194:6), a form of self-flattery or intellectual indulgence to which ignorance (and hence innocence) is especially susceptible. "He that know's nothing," Butler

wrote, "knows as little of himself, and ha's no more Sense of his own
defects then he has of any thing else which renders him impregnable
against all conviction, which no reason can promise it self" (63). Far
from suffering an eclipse, then, "the eies of Adam's understanding"
were for the first time opened at the Fall. This is not to say that Butler
believed Paradise well lost. Perhaps he would have if Adam had not
forfeited the tree, "the most compendious way of attaining" knowledge, along with the garden (19). But, in affording man the means of
acquiring knowledge himself, the tree also laid upon him the God-like
responsibility of distinguishing between truth and falsehood, and this,
from Butler's point of view, was an extremely difficult task for human
sense and reason.

Thus, according to Butler, God sentenced only certain men to physical labor; certain others (those endowed with particular intellectual
abilities) he sentenced to mental labor, to "Study, observation, and
Practice" in "as hard and barren a Soyl" as the earth was to those
condemned to physical punishment (19). Henceforth, man would purchase knowledge as well as bread by his own efforts; he would become
"a Slave to his own condition . . . forcd to drudge for that Food and
Cloathing which other creatures receive freely from the Bounty of
Nature" (82:4). This passage, included under the rubric "Nature" in
Butler's prose observations, refers, of course, to man's physical difficulties; there are other passages, however, that refer to the spiritual and
intellectual difficulties he shall encounter. A note in the manuscript
commonplace book (and then incorporated in the "Satyr Upon the
Imperfection and Abuse of Human Learning, Part 1st") about the
fruitless pains of linguistic study in the sciences continues as follows:

the variation of Languages at the Building of Babell was but a 2d Curse upon
the fall of man And as the first brought him knowledge at the Charge of
Labour and Drudgery in tilling the Earth that was renderd Barren of purpose
only to find him worke and in the End to devoure Him, So do's this 2d of
learning Languages afford him a very pittiful Returne of Knowledge in comparison of the intollerable Paines and Industry that is spent upon It; for which
hee would have nothing but his Labour for his Paines, if hee did not Divert
himselfe with setting false Values upon some little Things. . . .

(257)

In a section of the prose observations entitled "Wit and Folly," Butler
remarks that, after nature gave men reason, she provided them with

"neither Food, nor Cloaths, nor Armes (as she has don Beasts at her own Charge) but such as they can invent, and prepare for themselves" (56:2); and, under "Learning and Knowledge," he observes that men "do but more plainly perceive, their own wants and Nakednes, as he [i.e., Adam] did, which before in the State of Ignorance [Butler's phrase for "the State of Innocence"], were hidden from him, untill the eies of his understanding were opened, only to let him see his losses, and the Miseries which he had betrayd himself unto" (15:4).

But the bitter realization of human imperfection was, for Butler, only a part of the intellectual punishment of fallen man. Indeed, if Adam's first rational perception was of his "own wants and Nakedness," one of his first rational acts must have been his invention of clothing to conceal these truths about his nature. Like "a spruce Gallant," Butler notes, man "take's his cloaths for the better Part of his Redemption; For as Adam after his Fall among his other Defects found himself Naked (of which he appeared to be most Sensible and hid himself) So his Restoration from that Calamity, and Improvement of it into Bravery, cannot but apeare to him to be his greatest Indulgence" (196:3). These "indulgences"—the "setting [of] false values upon some little Things," as he described them in his note on the pains of linguistic study—Butler regarded as the causes of strife in scholarship, theology, and law. Thus, man himself deliberately confounds truth and falsehood, and in so doing he becomes the agent of his own punishment.

We may learn more of Butler's view of the intellectual punishment of fallen man by paying closer attention, therefore, to those passages in his writing which refer to clothing or to its absence. Sartorial ineptness and extravagance have of course always been commonplaces of comedy: in Butler's works we think of the inventory of Hudibras's external accoutrements, of the attention to dress in the prose Characters (two of which, the "Huffing Courtier" and the "Fantastic," are wholly delineated in these terms), and in the "Satyr on Our Ridiculous Imitation of the French." But such details do more than merely caricature extremes of fashion, for Hudibras's hose conceal that common human need that conventional literary knights of the road seem able to ignore: "He alwayes chose / To carry Vittle in his hose" (1:1, ll. 315–16); and the "Huffing Courtier"—who is the latest creation of his tailor—finds in clothes the regeneration of his original nature: "He is very careful to discover the Lining of his Coat, that you may not suspect any Want of Integrity or Flaw in him from the Skin outwards" (*Characters,* 70).

"Clothing," writes Paul Fussell in his study of Augustan humanism, "is the achievement of civilization, but the achievement of a high civilization is the creation of a symbolic clothing of conventions and institutions."[5] Like Jonathan Swift, Butler traced the moral and intellectual history of man in his creation of symbolic clothing; learned languages, "hard" words, cant, cabalistical and legal terms, literature, myth, religions, philosophical systems, and, especially, individual opinions—all are metaphorically treated in terms of clothing. But whereas the humanists regarded such clothing as the "motive of noble and social action,"[6] Butler saw it as the motive of deception and hypocrisy, as the occasion for many of those difficult judgments which "so fruitfully stocked" the world of knowledge after the Fall.

Butler would have agreed with the humanists that clothing (in both the literal and symbolic sense) was indispensable in a world from which God had withdrawn his providential care of man. The "Taylers Trad," he noted under the rubric "Contradictions," was instituted "by God almighty him self, for wee read in the Scripture, that he made cloaths for Adam and Eve of the skins of Beasts" (175:6); and, as we shall see, Butler himself regarded wit and fancy as "the Cloaths, and Ornaments of Judgment" (58:1). In such cases, a clear distinction is drawn between clothes and the thing clothed: Adam's suit did not alter his essential frailty; and true wit is made to contribute to "the Benefit and advantage of [the] Truth" it adorns (65:1). But again like Swift, Butler felt that this distinction was frequently ignored. Just as Gulliver used clothing to conceal his kinship with the Yahoos, so most men have turned this sign of their fallen condition to their own credit, "as if they gained not lost by it, and had made themselves finer then ever God meand they should bee" (234:1). Thus, Butler wrote in the "Satyr upon the Weakness and Misery of Man":

> Our *Bravery*'s but a vain Disguise,
> To hide us from the World's Eyes,
> The Remedy of a Defect,
> With which our Nakedness is deckt;
> Yet makes us swell with Pride, and boast,
> As if w' had gain'd by being lost.
>
> (*Satires*, 36)

And, as the means of satisfying the human desire to think well of oneself also serve the desire to be thought well of by others, men soon learned to cover the "Lineing" of vice worn "next their Bodys, for ease and convenience" with an outer dress of virtue "for shew" (74:4).

Butler frequently drew upon this contrast between the outer and inner man (symbolically, the clothed and unclothed man), the most obvious instance occurring in part 2 of *Hudibras,* where the knight, who falsely claims to have endured a whipping for his mistress, fears that she will "make me pull my *Dublet* off" (2:3, l. 82) and uncover the truth. Clothed, Hudibras appears as the champion of "*Faith,* and *Love,* and *Honour*"; stripped, he "shall be reduc'd t'a Knight oth' Post," that is, a professional perjurer (2:3, ll. 87–88). "All Bewty, and the Ornaments of it," Butler observed in perhaps the most Swiftian passage in the prose observations, "are Naturally designed for the outsides of things, and not their inward Parts: For if the Inside of the Bewtifullest Creature in the World were turned outward, nothing could appear more Gastly, and horrible" (96:1).

Not merely the conventional image of the dishonest tradesman prompted, therefore, Butler's characterization of the tailor as one who "Came in with the Curse; and is younger Brother unto Thorns, and Thistles, and Death"—a passage that continues by saying that, "if *Adam* had not fallen, he had never sat crossleg'd," and that "Sin and he [the tailor] are Partners" (*Characters,* 174). Clearly, in such references, the fashioning of clothes symbolizes the fallen condition of man—not only the *original error* caused by Adam's innocence, but also the perpetuation of the human tendency to deceive and be deceived that is occasioned by man's use of reason. Nevertheless, reason is, paradoxically, the only means by which error may be avoided and truth attained.

## Human Nature

This view of the paradoxical condition of "rational" man is the basis of Butler's theories of human nature and knowledge. Fallen mankind, he suggests, both in the prose observations and, implicitly, in the prose Characters, consists largely of knaves (those who employ reason to deceive others) and of the ignorant (those who are rationally deceived by knaves or by themselves). Fools and madmen comprise a third category of quasi-humanity: those creatures who—either through natural privation or accidental impairment (57:2)—lack the rational means of determining their proper places in the order of nature. Like the "natural" fool in Shakespeare's *King Lear,* the fools and madmen of this third group possess, Butler suggests, a special license (which the rationally

endowed ignorant are denied) to pursue their delusions: "That Providence," he notes, "that Cloaths, and Feede's Beasts, because they know
not how to help themselves, Provide's for all Sorts of Fooles, that are
aequally in capable of Relieving themselves without it" (58:3). Moreover, what little wit a fool has "tends naturally to knavery, and he is
dishonest by instinct" (*Characters,* 275). Natural fools (and madmen),
then, survive in a world where reason is perverted into fraud, and where
knavery becomes a "rational" science—the "Mechanics of Cheat" and
the "mathematical Magic of Imposture," as Butler calls it in the Character of "A Knave" (214). In the symbolic clothing of the church, the
courts, the various trades, and, of course, the underworld, such knavery
appeals (often in extremely subtle ways) to rational man's capacity for
incomplete knowledge and for self-approving "opinion"—to his *ignorance,* the word by which Butler distinguishes fallen man's tendency to
err from the original folly that led an innocent Adam to believe he was
God's equal. Butler therefore regarded knavery as "a just Judgment,
sent into this World to punish the Confidence and Curiosity of Ignorance, that out of a natural Inclination to Error will tempt its own
Punishment, and help to abuse itself" (*Characters,* 171).

But the ignorant also directly deceive themselves. Rejecting the
instruction of experience as prejudicial, such men have lost Eden for
nothing (76:2); and they remain, in spite of the divine direction to
study, observe, and practice, as liable to "venture beyond [their] Latitude" as any fool or madman (18:2). The latter, Butler believed, are
governed by the imagination, that "Sayle" of the understanding that is
"apt to receive, and be carry'd away with every winde of vanity, unles it
be stear'd" by reason, its "only Helme" (65:2). On the other hand,
reason, which was given to man for self-knowledge, will produce its
own illusions unless it submit its conceptions to "the Judgment, and
Arbitration of Sense" (62). Since man's "natural affectation" [*sic*] for
himself makes objective introspection impossible (for "no Man can
possibly be a Competent Judge of his own Conceptions, unless he cou'd
have more Reason than he has" [6:3]), his only dependable means to
knowledge lies in externals, in the empirical evidence of natural order
and of his own place within that order. Wanting this recourse to the
sensuous nature of things, or, where that is unobtainable, to "collaterall
Precedents, and Paralels from such as may be" (82:3), reason produces
not truth, but "speculation," a word that Butler uses (see Latin *specu-
lum*) in the sense of "mirror" (7:5); therefore, the "notions" of the
speculative reason reflect not nature (80:1), but the mind's own desires
(18:1). Without sense, Butler observed, reason is like a glass eye

"which though it cannot see, can make a Show as if it did, and is proof against al those accidents that use to destroy true ones" (63). For this reason, he believed, "al Ignorant People, are . . . naturally obstinate, in all things which they believe they know, only because they know nothing to the Contrary" (62).

To the partiality of such speculation, Butler traced much of the contentiousness of human learning. Theology that ignores the empirical evidence of "the Booke of Nature" and philosophy—both ancient and modern—are "speculative" in Butler's sense of the word. The philosopher described in his *Characters* makes hypotheses "as a Taylor does a Doublet without Measure, no Matter whether they fit *Nature,* he can make *Nature* fit them" (94). Aristotle, Butler noted elsewhere, studied nature "more in the metaphysiques of his own Braine, then her own certaine operations; As if his chiefest care had been to make his Systemes . . . agree among themselves very prettily, but perhaps without any great regard to Truth or Nature" (132:4). Democritus's mechanistic theory could have been "hit upon" only by one "mad enough to put out his owne eies" in order "that he might contemplate the better" (203:2); and the rationalist Descartes, whose distrust of both received philosophy and the delusive effects of sense led to his purging of all but self-evident truths from the mind, erred in believing the intellect "so cleare, and Infallible" that it did not require the "more Authenticall" test of sense (82:3).

But not even the senses are able to counteract the human tendency to err. Butler's most elaborate illustration of the mastery of sense by ignorance and opinion (in his sense of these terms) is made at the expense of seventeenth-century science, in "The Elephant in the Moon," a farcical tale he carried out in both tetrameter and pentameter versions. Like Swift, Butler was critical of the impracticalities of modern science, its exhibitionism, and its apparent refusal to direct its own efforts by commonsense standards of value. His general attitude toward such efforts may perhaps be inferred from the fact that he endowed Hudibras with scientific knowledge:

> . . . he by *Geometrick* scale
> Could take the size of *Pots of Ale;*
> Resolve by Sines and Tangents straight,
> If *Bread* or *Butter* wanted weight;
> And wisely tell what hour o'th' day
> The Clock does strike, by Algebra.
> (1:1, ll. 121–26)

In the fragmentary "Satyr upon the Royal Society" (Lamar's title),
Butler assembled a similar list of "occupations" for its members:

> To measure *Wind,* and weigh the *Air,*
> And turn a *Circle* to a *Square;*
> To make a *Powder of the Sun,*
> By which all Doctors should b' undone
> To find the *North-west* Passage out,
> Although the farthest Way about.
>
> (*Satires,* 33)

The end of true knowledge, Butler believed, was a simple and modest
one: the understanding of "what is Fit to be don" (11:7), as he stated it
in the prose observations. "Things that ly far of[f] the Sense" (83:3)
need not be known at all, and nature adapted human vision accordingly. But developments in optical science had removed this natural
safeguard, and opened to men a limitless sphere for worthless speculation and error.

The limits that Butler set to human knowledge need to be kept in
mind when we consider recent claims that his satires of science are not
antiscientific, but that, in fact, he absorbed a "fundamentally optimistic epistemology" from the "Baconian tendencies in the thought of his
time." "Far from [being] anti-science," William C. Horne has recently
written, "Butler's concern in . . . ["The Elephant in the Moon"] is very
much an echo of the cautions of the Royal Society scientists themselves"; and, to buttress a reading of the implied "positives" in the same
poem, Ken Robinson points to the verbal echoes, in Butler's prose
observations, of Bacon's *Advancement of Learning,* noting especially the
occurrence of a mirror image in the latter: "God hath framed the mind
of man as a mirror or glass, capable of the image of the universal
world."[7] Butler did accept the reports of the senses as the basis of
knowledge, but after asserting that "all knowledge is nothing but a
right observation of Nature," he went on to elaborate upon the human
impossibility of achieving that "right" observation (19). He does appear
to have picked up Bacon's image of the mind as a mirror but, as often as
not, proceeds to turn it into an image of error, an instrument of
distortion or of intellectual self-approval ("Speculations," he observes,
"use us as glasses, and deliver that Right in appearance that proves left
in tryal" [7:5]); or, if not that, mirrors occur with an implicit warning
concerning their use: "the Minde and understanding of Man is but a

Mirror, that receive's, and Represents, the Images of those Objects that Nature set's before it at a just Distance, as far as it is able to receive them, and therefore the more remote things are, the more uncapable it is to entertaine them; and if it ever hap to be in the Right, it is like a lucky cast at Dice, but by mere chance, and Hap-hazzard" (80:2).

The "positives" of "The Elephant in the Moon" are difficult to establish. Simple inversion of the "negatives" seems to beg the question, formalizing the behavior of the virtuosos as "bad scientific procedure" in order to predicate Butler's advocacy of a properly scientific one. But whatever this satire has to say about scientific procedure, its obvious joke is that men make mountains out of molehills—the virtuosos or dilettantes of a "Learn'd *Society*" make a lunar elephant out of an earthly mouse. That Butler's virtuosos seem especially prone to this tendency to enlarge upon things is due, at least in part, to their use of instruments of magnification (an issue perhaps brought into sharper focus as the poem evolved by the currency of a controversy over the validity of telescopic evidence waged in 1670 and 1671 by Henry Stubbe and Joseph Glanville[8]). Butler's primary concern, however, is with the general ethical issue of man's attitude toward falsehood and truth—specifically, with his use of reason to cultivate falsehood and to subvert truth in the interest of self-esteem. The poem describes the behavior of a group of virtuosos who one evening turn their telescope upon the moon—which they assume to be inhabited—and observe (or believe they observe) the inhabitants engaged in a war. Then,

> . . . a stranger Sight appears
> Than e're was seen in all the Spheres,
> A Wonder more unparalel'd,
> Than ever mortal Tube beheld;
> An *Elephant* from one of those
> Two mighty Armies is broke loose.
> (11. 121–26)

In great excitement the observers agree "to draw an exact Narrative" of their observations; and, while they are engrossed in this work, the footboys take their turn at the telescope. With eyes unclouded by vanity or by learned hypotheses—with little more than "Monkey Ingenuity"—they promptly identify the lunar armies as "swarms of flies and gnats" and the elephant as a mouse that had "gotten in / The hollow tube" (11. 353–54).

The poem presents, then, two "discoveries": an elephant on the moon, and a mouse in a telescope. The first discovery (together with the incorrect identification of insects as warring armies) is anticipated—the hypostatized end of a long sequence of non sequiturs, circular reasonings, and deductions from invalid assumptions. Sensitive to the public ridicule of their past experiments, the virtuosos seize upon the notion of a lunar war as the means of improving the image of the Society. No longer, says the chief spokesman for the group (Robert Boyle, perhaps),

> . . . shall our ablest *Virtuosos*
> Prove Arguments for Coffee-houses
> . . . . . . . . . . .
> Nor shall our past Misfortunes more
> Be charg'd upon the ancient Score:
> . . . . . . . . . . .
> This one Discovery's enough,
> To take all former Scandals off.
>                              (ll. 205–26)

The second discovery (that of the mouse, or *truth*) is resisted and is reasoned against by the members of the Society; at one point, it is suggested that "the Cause of th' *Elephant,* or *Mouse*" be decided by ballot, that the virtuosos "find, or make, the Truth by Votes" (1. 476). When an earlier observation casts some doubt upon the existence of the elephant, each virtuoso is "Resolv'd . . . to make [the discovery] good . . . And rather his own Eyes condemn / Than question what h' had seen with them" (ll. 257–60). But what had the virtuosos seen? The elephant is not a perception at all; it is a rational invention, a "speculation." Thus, one of Butler's virtuosos triumphantly concludes that the existence of "*Elephants* . . . in the *Moon* / Though we had now discover'd none, / Is easily made manifest" (ll. 145–47).

The self-delusiveness of human nature is, of course, exaggerated for comic effect in "The Elephant in the Moon," and it is easy to overextend the application of the satire. Butler was a proponent of neither skepticism—"the Modern Fals-doctrine of the Court"—nor anti-intellectualism, an attitude he associated with the enthusiastic or fanatic religious sects. "If there be no Art to improve the understanding of Man," he argues in one of the prose observations, "there can be no Improvement of any thing else"; and if the understanding "cannot help it selfe, it is below the Ingenuity of Beasts that are capable of being taught to do many things which Nature never bred them up to" (18). *There,* perhaps, is the "positive" in Butler's satire of science: human nature *may* be improved because man is *animal rationis capax.* But that optimism does not lessen his distrust of the intellectual effort to improve man's own and others' opinions of himself. Truth, he believed, exists; but as truth wants "that free latitude to flourish in, which error always usurpes" (24:3), men frequently avoid it. A more complete statement of this idea is made by another of the virtuosos (probably Robert Hooke) in "The Elephant in the Moon." When the footboys innocently uncover the fact that the elephant is in truth a mouse, the virtuoso remarks that

> . . . Truth is too reserv'd, and nice,
> T' appear in mix'd Societies;
> Delights in solit'ary Abodes,
> And never shews her self in Crowds;
> A sullen little Thing, below
> All Matters of Pretence and Show;
>
> . . . . . . . . . .
>
> For, what has Mankind gain'd by knowing
> His little Truth, but his Undoing,
> Which wisely was by Nature hidden,
> And only for his Good forbidden?
> And, therefore, with great Prudence does
> The World still strive to keep it close;
> For if all secret Truths were known,
> Who would not be once more undone?
> For Truth has always Danger in't,
> And here, perhaps, may cross some Hint,
> We have already agreed upon . . .
>                    (ll. 405–10, 419–29)

The virtuoso speaks for himself and his colleagues in the "Learn'd *Society*" of Butler's satire, but he also voices Butler's misgivings about the society of all rational men who are united in the common effort to subvert any truth that threatens to diminish their self-esteem.

## Poetry

Butler's awareness of the human tendency to ignore unflattering truth was also an important determinant of his views on poetry: if men can tamper with their own consciences (as is implied in the final lines of the passage last quoted), it is doubtful that they will respect the truths offered by another—even when, as tradition held, that other was divinely inspired. Butler himself did not take this exalted view of the poet—as readers familiar with the invocation of the muse in *Hudibras* will know. His prose observations include relatively few comments on poetry or its authors; and those we find (an approving reference to Ben Jonson [128:1] is a noteworthy exception) tend to be adversely critical. He regarded verse as a counterfeit and deviant mode of expression—having "something in the Stamp and Coyne, to answer for the Allay, and want of Intrinsique Value"—and, believing it "harder to imitate Nature then any Deviation from her," he argued that "Prose require's a more Proper and Natural Sense, and expression then verse" (138:1). Like Swift, Butler distrusted serious poetry, for he associated fancy (which in devoted circles was considered "inspiration" or wit) with religious enthusiasm and madness. His satirical Character of "A Small Poet" likens its subject to the "*Fanatic,* that inspires himself with his own Whimsies" (82); and one of his prose observations states that "Gifts and wit are but a kind of Hotheadednes, that Renders those that are Possest with it, better at Extempore, then Premeditation . . ." (187:2). The poet Sir John Denham's recovery from madness—which Butler celebrated in a mock "Panegyric"—provided the perfect opportunity to make this point:

> Sir, you've outliv'd so desperate a Fit,
> As none could do, but an immortal Wit;
> Had yours been less, all Helps had been in vain,
> And thrown away, tho' on a less sick Brain:
> But you were so far from receiving Hurt,
> You grew improv'd, and much the better for't.
>                                              (*Satires,* 120)

Butler subscribed to a conservative aesthetic that regarded true wit as the product of both judgment and fancy; judgment, Hobbes declared, produced "the strength and structure," fancy "the Ornaments of a Poem."[9] The same point is made even more explicitly when Butler counsels men to "make Truth and observation the Ground and Foundation, or rather the end of their Studys, and use Fancy, and Stile only as Instrumentall, to expresse their Conceptions the more easily, and Naturally . . ." (69:2). Butler further defined "wit" as a "slight of the

Minde" that "deliver's things otherwise then they are in Nature, by rendring them greater or lesse then they really are (which is cal'd Hyperbole) or by putting them into some other condition then Nature ever did (as when the Performances of Sensible and Rationall Beings are apply'd to Senseles and Inanimate things, with which the writings of Poets abound)" (64:1). "Style" he defined as the "proper naturall and Significant way of expressing our Conceptions in words, and as it agree's or disagree's with those is either good or Bad" (144:1). According to these definitions, "wit" is purely mental, a conceptualizing of actual things; "style" is verbal, a way of expressing these conceptions. And while wit knowingly produces distorted conceptions of things, style—like "truth" itself (the congruity between the mental images of things and the disposition of those things in nature)—aims at a congruity between conceptions and the words expressing them.

It will readily be seen that the "slight of Minde" to which Butler likened wit is similar to that human tendency to deceive that he decried at other places in his prose observations and in "The Elephant in the Moon." Although it was probably already a convention by Butler's time, clothing—his symbol of the means of that deception—is also a common analogy for wit in his writing. Hudibras, we remember, seemed "loath to wear . . . out" his wit and therefore used it only "on Holy-dayes, or so, / As men their best Apparel do" (1:1, ll. 47–50). The "Small Poet" of the Characters is described as a "Haberdasher" who makes the most of his "very small Stock" of wit through thrift, theft, and rhetorical substitutes (82). Similarly, writers who are given to obscurities of style are likened to "Citizens that commonly choose the Darkest streets to set up in, or make false lights that the Spots and Steines of their Stuffs may not be perceived" (132). Just as fallen man uses reason to create a false paradise, the "Small Poet" uses wit to project a vanished Golden Age upon the present Age of Iron, converting men into heroes and women into nymphs (86). Thus the virtuosos in "The Elephant in the Moon" attempt to narrow the credibility gap created in their hoax by calling upon one,

> . . . who for his Excellence
> In height'ning Words and shad'wing Sense,
> And magnifying all he writ
> With curious microscopick Wit,
> Was magnify'd himself no less.
>
> (ll. 167–71)

Butler did not, however, condemn all wit; "when it imploys those things which it borrows of Falshood, to the Benefit and advantage of Truth, as in Allegories, Fables, and Apologues, it is of excellent use," he believed, "as making a Deeper impression into the mindes of Men then if the same Truths were plainely deliverd" (65:1), for wit has the power of raising the passions and of short-circuiting reason and judgment to excite the will directly (65:2). Moreover, since wit is "capable of Prodigie and strangnes, and of neare kin to a Ly which . . . [men] have ever been naturally inclynd to," it is a better means of teaching moral truths than either reason or precept (8:3). Even in political action, Butler recognized the advantages of wit over reason. The "chiefest Art of Government," he noted, is the ability "to convert the Ignorance, Folly, and Madness of Mankinde . . . to their own good, which can never be don, by telling them Truth and Reason . . . but by little Tricks and Devises (as they cure Madmen) . . ." (112:7). The poet too, if he employs wit "to the Benefit and advantage of Truth" (that is, if he uses fancy to clothe the truth), may, we should conclude, be able to deceive men for their own good.

Though Butler's conception of fancy as a mere instrument for expressing truth is a critical commonplace of neoclassicism, little else in his critical pronouncements justifies this label. That stubborn adherence to the facts of experience that prevented his endorsing the theoretical justification of rational man tended also to invalidate any rational system for judging literature. The nature exalted in neoclassical criticism was, in part at least, the Aristotelian nature that moved always away from accidents and toward perfection. Such a view did not ignore empirical reality—the accidental world of phenomena—but its preference for intellectually conceived perfection is clearly apparent in the doctrine of poetic kinds that sanctioned realism only at a specified distance from the more respected forms of tragedy and epic. But, for Butler, the "truths" that his age found embodied in the heroic fictions of the higher genres were flattering ameliorations that contradicted the picture of man and his world acquired through sense and experience. To Butler, the modern writer of romance who follows the practice of the ancient heroic poets "Pulls down old Histories to build them up finer again, after a new Model of his own designing," and he "takes away all the Lights of Truth in History to make it the fitter tutoress of Life" (*Characters,* 169). There remains only one decorum of practical value to the modern writer of heroics, Butler ironically concludes, and that is "in dating his Histories in the Days of old, and putting all his own Inventions upon ancient Times; for when the World was younger, it might, perhaps, love, and fight, and do generous Things at the Rate he describes them; but since it is grown old, all these heroic Feats are laid by and utterly given over, nor ever like to come in fashion again" (*Characters*, 169). The decorum of heroic literature, the suiting of a grand style to a great subject, merely conceals the essential inconsistency of human nature.

A similar criticism is made of the classical decorum of tragedy, which, from Butler's point of view, also affirmed a morality that could only appear arbitrary when judged by the circumstances of real life. One of the specific targets in Butler's satire "Upon Critics Who Judge of Modern Plays Precisely by the Rules of the Ancients"—a general attack upon the abstract morality of Thomas Rymer's *Tragedies of the Last Age* (1677)—was Aristotle's prescription that tragedy arouse both pity and fear in the spectator, and (since pity is generated by undeserved misfortune and fear by the misfortune of those like ourselves) that the tragic protagonist be neither eminently evil nor eminently good. Grounding his own views in a common sense that does not depend upon rules or models, Butler argued that "no Affliction can terrify others from the like, but where it is Justly Deservd," just as "none can move Compassion, that is not Injustly incurd"—neither of these effects being possible in Aristotle's characters of "Midling Sizes" (186). In other words, the Aristotelian rules governing plot and character destroy what Butler regarded as the didactic design of the dramatic fable:

> No longer shal Dramatiques be confind
> To draw tru Images, of al Mankinde,
> To Punish in Effigie Criminals,
> Reprieve the Innocent, and hang the False;
> But a Club-Law [to] execute, and kill,
> For nothing, whom so ere they Please, at will:
> To terrify Spectators from committing
> The Crimes, they did, and sufferd for, unwitting.
>                                    (*Satires*, 61)

In Rymer's rules of correctness, Butler saw another instance of the deceptiveness of reason unqualified by the senses or, in this case, by feeling. Rymer, he believed, allowed his head to rule his heart; he tried to judge—as the title of Butler's satire puts it—"*Precisely* by the Rules of the Ancients," using as it were an instrument of science—"Cylinders of Torricellian Glasses" (a barometer)—to measure "the Aire upon Pernassus" (ll. 15–16). What was inimical to reason, Rymer ignored.

This tendency to ignore what does not fit, to lose perspective in too narrow a focus, characterizes much of what Butler targeted in his satire. This is not to say that the project of his satire—or of Restoration satire generally, according to Kevin Cope—simply sets experience against ideal truth: that would make experience itself susceptible to satiric attack. Butler observed that "right reason" consists "in an impartiall examination of *all extreames,* and a giving right Judgment upon *both sides;* but he whose latitude is not able to extend so far, but is wholly taken up with *any one, will never understand the Truth of either*" (62—my italics). Cope concludes from this statement that truth, for the Restoration satirist, "consists in the process of understanding and judging dichotomies, not in the dichotomies themselves. Truth is a latitude, a range, an openness; it is not the sharp categories of right and wrong, true and false, or even confidently held ideal and butt of satire."[10] Michael Seidel arrives at a similar position when he remarks that "For Butler, perspective is an essential quality for the man and the satirist hoping to avoid not only his deception by others, but self-deception as well. The satirist must at least pose as an objectivist if he is to manipulate his own variety of artistic distortion."[11] The result of this openness and range is satire and criticism that appear to reject norms. Butler judged not only the hypocrisy of Cromwell's Commonwealth, but the inverted hypocrisy of Charles's Restoration, and he exhibited a similar impartiality as a critic. He condemned not only the stylistic excess of metaphysical wit as poetic pretense, but found the new rhetorical wit of antithesis an even more accessible counterfeit for true poetry: the former, he remarked in the Character of "A Quibbler," "is already cried down, and the other . . . the only Elegance of our modern Poets . . . having nothing in it but *Easiness,* and being never used by any lasting Wit will in wiser Times fall to nothing of itself" (133).

What most sharply differentiates Butler's views on literature from those of the neoclassical critics is this refusal to reconcile the differences between poetic truth and real knowledge. In *An Essay on Criticism,* for instance, Alexander Pope remarks that although "wit and judgment often are at strife," they are "meant to be each other's aid, like man and wife," and implies that in the best literary practice wit and judgment are in fact reconciled. Those *"nameless Graces"* that lie "beyond the Reach of Art" do not invalidate his system; they simply stand outside it. For Butler, however, no such accommodation was possible: though "there is no tru wit that is not produc'd by a great Deal of Judgment," wit (or fancy in this context) and reason (or judgment) "will [n]ever be brought to stand in Tune together" (58:2). True wit is always mysterious; there is no rational justification for it: the best wits, Butler notes, "have just confidence enough to keep them from utterly Renouncing" their wit, "which they are apt to do upon the smallest Check, if something else then their own Inclinations did not oppose them in it" (56:1). This confidence (just sufficient, we should note), he regarded as the true "Poeticall Fury" (60); and it was to be found significantly, not in the heroic but in the comic genres, and particularly in satire. In fact, Butler completely inverted the traditional hierarchy of poetic kinds by setting above the heroic poem even the often judiciously condemned lampoon which, "if rightly considered," is "capable of doing Princes more good [than flattering panegyrics] . . . and like Charmes easily cure those Fantastique Distempers in Governments, which being neglected grow too stubborn to obey any but as Rigid Medecines" (163:2).

The "something else" that opposes the satirist's judgment is his anger, an emotion aroused by the folly and ignorance of the world. "It is difficult not to write satire," Juvenal wrote in his first satire; and Butler noted from the same source that "nothing . . . provokes and sharpens wit like Malice, and Anger" (59:3). Butler, in other words, justifies the license assumed by the witty satirist as a special decorum, the madness of the world having immunized itself to every corrective but a greater madness. Unlike the heroic poet, who is transported by a rapture of love for "what should be"—that other "kinde of Fooles Paradise" that is actually beneficial to folly and knavery (11:2)—the comic poet and satirist (Butler makes little distinction between the two) are imaginatively transported by a rapture of hatred for "what is." Satires, therefore, "that are only provok'd with the Madnes and Folly of the world, are found to containe more wit, and Ingenuity then all other writings whatsoever" (60), and whereas heroic poetry "handle's the slightest, and most Impertinent Follys . . . in a formall Serious and unnaturall way," comedy, burlesque, and satire handle "the most Serious matters in a Frolique and Gay humor, which has always been found the more apt to instruct . . ." (13.3). Even so, madness is a dangerous medicine; "notwithstanding the many Advantages that wit receives from Passion," Butler warned, "there is nothing in Nature so pernicious, and Distructive to all manner of Judgment" (61). What, then, prevents the angry satirist from becoming simply another madman? Michael Seidel explains that Butler held to an implicit distinction between *inherent madness*—an extravagant single-mindedness that makes one "solidly, and Profoundly mad," in Butler's words (57:2)—and *rhetorical madness*—a "systemized rage" that manages to maintain "a necessary perspective," again, the "objectivist pose" that protects the satirist from the constricted vision of "but one thing at once." "The maddened satirist and the mad world meet," Seidel says, "to produce a heightened form of negative energy, and this, after all, is why we thrill at the attack,"[12] or why, in Butler's words, the world "is always more delighted to heare the Faults and vices though of itself well describd, then all the Panegyriques that ever were" (60).

Experience had taught Butler that in real men the traditional attributes of literary greatness disguised qualities that were quite the reverse of those to which they were attached in tragedy and in the epic. The heroic ideal of honor, for instance, was for Butler (as for Falstaff) "a mere scutcheon," an empty term peddled by heralds (*Characters,* 116) and claimed by highwaymen (*Characters,* 279). At best, the word designated "a mere Negative Continence," as of women "only not being whores" (74:5). More frequently, Butler associated heroic honor with the stubbornness of the ignorant. Under the rubric "Opinion" in the prose observations, he wrote that "men of honor are in Probability the most like to take the worst Courses (if no other will Serve) to vindicate that Reputation, the Loss of which is So Grievious to them, and the shame so Intollerable" (80:2). In the prose observations and the Characters, the romantic images of honor are common analogies for the deception of self and others. Butler notes that the fashion of witty repartee is a "modern way of Running at Tilt," in which victory depends upon "Confidence" (arrogant self-conceit) as formerly it depended upon "the best Beaver" (219–20). His modern knights-errant may be found in the mock-Pindaric on "the Most Renouned Du-Vall" (a highwayman), and in such Characters as the "Hector," the "Anabaptist," the "Mountebank," and the "Opiniater," who, like the ignorant man, is pledged "by his Order to defend the weak and distressed" by delivering "enchanted Paradoxes" and obscurities from "invisible Castles" (220). No doubt recent history also contributed to the bankruptcy of the heroic ideal, for although "no Age ever abounded more with Heroical Poetry then the present, . . . there was never any wherein fewer Heroicall Actions were performd" (175:1). Butler had witnessed "two living burlesques," Ricardo Quintana has said: for "what had the Commonwealth been but a romance. . . . And if recent poets were to be believed, what was the Restoration period but an epic"?[13] Butler's observation on the Long Parliament demonstrates one half of this view: "The Long Parliament to secure the Liberties of the People from themselves, hid them in the invisible Hands of those Fayries the keepers of the Libertys. But Oliver stormd the Inchanted Castle, and tooke the Lady into his own Protection" (164:1).

That Butler should also use this devalued imagery to speak of the satirist is puzzling. "A Satyr," he wrote in one of the prose observations, "is a kinde of Knight Errant that goe's upon Adventures, to Relieve the Distressed Damsel Virtue, and Redeeme Honor out of Inchanted Castles, And opprest Truth, and Reason out of the Captivity of Gyants and Magitians: and though his meaning be very honest, yet some believe he is no wiser then those wandring Heros usd to be, though his Performances and Atchievments be ever so Renownd and Heroicall" (215:5). Ruth Nevo reads this passage as clear evidence of Butler's ambivalence about the heroic ideal—his use of it as "a mechanism of satiric contrast between superior and vulgar" which he then undermines because his "attitude is profoundly anti-heroic."[14] But the passage may also be read ironically, defining satire quixotically as a narrative mode "fated to wander and destined to do no good whatever." This is the view of Michael Seidel, who relates the fictive context of the satirist-errant to the satirist's objectivist "pose," an "extravagance" that assures satirical victories, but also suggests that "it is perhaps unwise to believe in their efficacy."[15] In a later comment on the passage, Seidel says that by "identifying the parodic basis of his effort, he [Butler] like Cervantes, links the satirist to the extravagancies of the satiric subject." "Satiric errantry," he declares, "is for Butler (as it was for Cervantes) an effect of lunatic singlemindedness."[16]

## Some Specific Views

If the author of *Hudibras* and "The Elephant in the Moon" is singleminded in his criticism of Puritanism and of science, the views of the author of the prose observations and the verse fragments that René Lamar gathered under the title "Poetical Thesaurus" resist easy classification. This fact will become apparent if we review a few of his prose and verse remarks on government and religion.

Coloring Butler's opinions on both these subjects is his frank acknowledgement of the chaotic state of the world of human affairs. Disorder is real, he suggests, an inalterable condition of human society that we can only try to come to terms with. Democracy, he wrote in the Character of "A Republican" is "the effect of a crazy brain" (59); and political theorists, like James Harrington and his fellow members of the Rota, are impractical dreamers; for, believing in words rather than things, they are unable to "understand the Difference between Specula-tion and Practice" (56). Even more concrete efforts to improve social institutions through political revolution or through religious reforma-tion were, he believed, certain to fail. The futility of such actions, Butler seems to say, is due to the impossibility of rational appeal—of reducing (as Swift put it in *A Tale of a Tub*) the notions of every member of society "exactly to the same Length, and Breadth, and Height" as that of the reformer, who must therefore use unjust means to achieve his ends. Butler, like Swift, also observed, in his Character of "A Humorist," the one exception to this rule: that if a madman "have the Luck to meet with many of [his] own temper, instead of being ridiculous, he becomes a Church" (190).

Thus, Butler maintained, rebellion is promoted "with nothing else but Lyes, and cheates and Impostures. For civil Armes can neither be raysd, nor maintaind, by honest meanes" (36). And, at another place, he contradicts the Hobbesian notion that a de facto government is a government de jure by observing that "an unjust Title [to a throne] cannot be supported but by unjust meanes. And for want of this all our late usurpations miscarrid" (114:1). In other words, the ruler who governs by an unjust claim must become a tyrant to maintain himself; and tyranny only incites further revolution. But this conclusion is a political fact that even princes with a just title to rule must recognize, none of whom, Butler maintained, "would deny his Subjects Liberty of Conscience if it were in his Power to grant it, without violating the Law of selve-preservation; for it being the Nature of all Sects (like other vermine) to increase and multiply, there is no Religion that can become the most Numerous but do's Naturally incline to suppress or destroy all others, and to give way to that, is to take part with such as indeavour to subvert the Government" (160:6). Monarchy, then, is no guarantee of civil order. Butler's "Satyr upon the Licentious Age of Charles the 2d," though primarily a moral rather than a political criticism of the Restora-tion, nevertheless makes the point that a justly ordained king, far from bringing "a just and active wisdom to direct the force of govern-ment",[17] has allowed men actively to seek disorder—"As if the Laws of Nature had been made / Of purpose, only to be disobey'd" (*Satires,* 42).

How, then, is civil order to be achieved? Should a king tyrannically oppose the forces of civil disorder, and run the risk of arousing open rebellion, or should he grant his subjects the liberty they crave and, in effect, voluntarily license the subversion or decay of his own government? Butler restated this question as a paradox in one of his verse fragments:

> . . . when a Nation is a Slave,
> What Crowns of Monarchs can be safe?
> And still the less we wast [demand] our Right
> W' Injoy the greater Freedom by't.
>
> (*Satires*, 441)

Rejecting the powers of both the king and the people, Butler here seems to place his faith in a self-regulating (or trimming) principle in the relations between rulers and the ruled. Again, in one of the prose observations, he wrote that "Governments are made like Naturall Productions by Degrees according as their Materials are brought in by time, and those Parts of it that are unagreeable to their Nature, cast of[f]" (113:1). Butler's references to processes of natural evolution in this passage adumbrate a theory of government as organism: "Governments like Natural Bodys have their times of growing Perfection and Declining, and according to their Constitutions, some hold out longer, and some decay sooner then other. . . ." The Character of "A Republican"—a Harringtonian engineer of government—makes the point even more clearly: "he forgets that no Government was ever made by model: For they are not built as Houses are, but grow as Trees do. And as some Trees thrive best in one Soil, some in another; so do Governments, but none equally in any, but all generally where they are most naturally produced" (56).

Butler's conception of government as a dynamic and changing organism, his rejection of the notion of a state as a static and inanimate structure that may be constructed from a blueprint, is another illustration of his distance from the more humanist stance of the Augustan thinkers. For them, nature was, in one sense, itself a grand blueprint or, in another sense, the "fabric" realized from that plan. Locke referred to the Deity as an "Architect," and Johnson spoke of the art of the mason as "one of the principal arts by which reasoning beings are distinguished from the brute" (*Adventurer*, no. 128). For such men, as Paul Fussell has pointed out, the contrast between the natural and the artificial, the animate and the inanimate, was felt as a difference between "the temporary and the permanent, the frail and the powerful, the puny and the majestic, the living thing that crawls the earth and the cold, lifeless thing that triumphs over gravitation and time."[18] Butler would have felt that such an attitude failed to account for the dynamics of human society, the *accidents* in nature that contradicted even God's plan—though not without His foreknowledge (33:5). In human affairs, it was the artificial, the abstract, and the inanimate that broke down. The mechanistic analogy used by Descartes to describe the mind, and by Hobbes to describe the state, served Butler only as a metaphor of folly and ignorance. But as an organism, the state was to Butler both susceptible to illness and able to restore itself to health and vigor. Permitted to develop naturally—without the revolutions of disgruntled elements in society, or the impositions of reforming theorists—the state will gradually adapt itself to the real conditions in which it must exist. In theory, Butler probably regarded the constitutional monarchy of the Restoration as such an evolving organism, for "among Governments," he wrote, "Monarchy has in the manage and practice of it more of Commonwealth, and Commonwealth more of Monarchy then either have of what they are cald. For noe Monarch can possibly Governe alone, but must of Necessity submit and be ruled by the advice, and Counsell of others" (170:3). And in this connection, he observed that "there is nothing in Nature more Arbitrary than a Parliament, and yet there is nothing Else that is able to preserve the Nation from being Govern'd by an Arbitrary Power, and confine Authority within a Limited Compass" (4:7). Quite literally, Butler's political philosophy was a science of dealing with the imperfect.

To this view of government as an organism may also be traced Butler's anti-Catholic and anti-Puritan positions, which are in large part political. The threat of Catholicizing England (of which he complains much more bitterly than of the Puritanizing of the nation) represented to him the transplanting of a foreign stock that was unnatural to the native climate and soil: the promoting of "the Interests of a forrein Prince; in opposition to our owne," and the removing of "the 'Staple of Religion, so well settled heere" (275:2). Popery—"having serv'd out an Apprenticeship to Tyranny, [and] as soon as it was out of its time . . . set up for itself"—evolved as a form of tyranny "most advantagious . . . to weake Princes" (4:8). Butler implies that the post-Reformation soil of England would reject the Roman transplant with all the consequent upheaval of a new reformation. Puritanism, on the other hand, quite obviously constituted an interruption of the natural evolution of English government. If Butler found the best features of a commonwealth in monarchy, he found the worst features

of monarchy in the Puritan commonwealth: "in the Senates of Repub-
liques some one Commonly governes all the rest, and has that really in
power, which Princes have but in Name" (170:3). Indeed, Butler saw
little difference between Catholic tyranny and Puritan tyranny.

Butler also considered the Catholic and the Puritan as theological
(or, better, psychological) brethren—an illustration of his assumption
that extremes meet. The ground of his criticism here was the irrationality of these religions—no real inconsistency with his criticism of the
unaided use of abstract reason implicit in his ethical and intellectual
views. At any rate, his insistence upon a reasonable basis for faith is one
of the few unequivocal positions he takes in his observations about
religion, which are virtually impossible to reduce to the tenets of a
recognizable denomination: "Faith can determine nothing of Reason,
but Reason can of Faith, and therefore if Faith be above Reason (as some
will have it) it must be reason only that can make it appeare to be
so . . . Faith cannot define Reason, but Reason can Faith, and therefore it should seeme to be the lardger" (67:1).

Such a statement does not, of course, make Butler a Deist; for
seventeenth-century Anglicanism had rationalist as well as fideist adher-
ents.[19] On the other hand, those marginal references, in his manuscript
commonplace book, to seventeenth-century English churchmen—
references which suggest to Norma Bentley that possibly "toward the
end of his life Butler found the Church of England more satisfying"—
may, as Hugh de Quehen even more plausibly suggests, be the nota-
tions of the manuscript's transcriber, William Longueville.[20] But if
Butler was a Deist, he was one who believed in the divinity of Christ:
"Hoc est Corpus meum, is true in a Litteral Sense," he writes in the
prose observations, "for as Bread naturally turne's to Flesh, and wine to
bloud; He, to whom all times are present, might very properly say that
is, that was to bee" (35:2).

Butler's Christianity rested upon the broadest possible basis. Since
"all men agree in the end of Religion that God is to be worshipd"
(32:4), "let all bee done out of *that only true Principle* of obedience; Love
to God; presented vnto Him upon *that only ground of Acceptation,* Jesus
Christ; & seasoned w$^{th}$ that Acceptable Grace, Humility."[21] The point
is that Butler was not interested in the doctrinal opinions that account
for denominational distinctions; nor did he believe that God was interested in them any "further then they conduce to . . . [men's] own
Peace and Quietnes" (165:1).

# Chapter Three
# *Hudibras*

## History

Butler described the genesis of the first part of *Hudibras* in his letter of 19 March 1662/3, to Sir George Oxenden. Around 1659 he had become acquainted, he wrote, with "a West Countrey $Kn^t$ then a Coll: in the Parliament Army & a $Com^{te}$ man" who had lodged in the same house with him in Holbourne; and, finding "his humor soe pleasant," he endeavored (almost fortuitously, he suggests) "to render his Character as like as I could." Sir Hudibras's squire, Ralpho, the letter continues, was modeled on a clerk employed by Butler's fellow lodger,

> an $Independ^t$, betweene whome, & $y^e$ $Kn^t$, there fell out Such perpetuall disputes about Religion, as you will find up & downe in $y^e$ Booke for as neere as I could I sett downe theire very words. As for $y^e$ Story I had it from $y^e$ $Kn^{ts}$ owne Mouth, & is so farr from being feign'd, $y^t$ it is upon Record, for there was a Svite of Law upon it betweene $y^e$ $Kn^t$, & $y^e$ Fidler, in $w^{ch}$ $y^e$ $K^{nt}$ was overthrowne to his great shame, & discontent, for $w^{ch}$ he left $y^e$ Countrey & came up to Settle at London.

Butler denied any deeper level of historical reference in the poem, remarking yet that his "chiefe designe was onely to give $y^e$ world a Just $Acco^t$ of $y^e$ Ridiculous folly & Knavery of $y^e$ Presbiterian & Independent Factions then in power. . . ."[1]

We have no reason to doubt Butler's identification of the originals of Sir Hudibras and Ralpho, nor to question his statement that *Hudibras* was originally conceived as a comic reworking of a real dispute between an overzealous Presbyterian magistrate and an overexuberant merrymaker (overexuberant at least by Puritan standards): the poem ends, we may recall, with a court action initiated by the knight. If such a motivating incident seems rather trivial, we need only recall Parliament's closing of the theaters and its curtailment of public amusements—including even traditional Christmas festivities—in the 1640s to find historical precedents. The Puritans themselves conceived of their zeal for piety—

the special gift of God to a chosen few—as a sort of romantic *gloire,* and they practiced and cultivated it with all the seriousness that a medieval knight dedicated to his chivalric calling. Butler had only to exploit the comic possibilities in these materials, to portray his West Country magistrate and clerk as a latter-day Don Quixote and Sancho Panza, and to depict their legal entanglement with a fiddler as a Puritan-tilting-at-windmills—inspired, however, by self-interested materialism rather than by idealism or religious fervor. Butler named his hero Hudibras, after the "sterne melancholy" lover of the pleasure-hating Elissa of Spenser's *Faerie Queene,* Sir Huddibras, a knight "not so good of deedes, as great of name . . . more huge in strength, than wise in workes" (*FQ* 2:1, l. 17) and one whose effort to make "peace is but continuall iarre" (*FQ* 2:1, l. 26).[2] To Hudibras's squire, Butler gave the name Ralph or, depending on poetic exigencies, Ralpho or Raph, perhaps after the hero of Francis Beaumont's *Knight of the Burning Pestle,* probably also the inspiration for the occupational names of the individual bearbaiters (Trulla, Crowdero, Orsin, etc.)[3]; and, to the original "story" of the knight and the fiddler, he supplied (if they were not part of the historical incident) a company "such as Commonly make up Bearebaitings."[4]

As we shall see, Cervantes and Spenser contributed more to *Hudibras* than models and names for its protagonists. Don Quixote, his squire, Sancho Panza, and his mistress, Dulcinea del Toboso, are specifically mentioned in the poem (1:2, ll. 310, 873; 2:1, l. 876), and Butler may have gotten the idea for a number of its incidents (e.g., the whipping, the skimmington, the masquerade) from Cervantes's novel. No doubt other works also stimulated Butler's invention: Rabelais's *Gargantua and Pantagruel,* the *Satyr Menippée,* and Sir John Mennis and James Smith's *Wit Restor'd* (1658) have been suggested—and more recently, *The Diarium* (1656) by Butler's contemporary, Richard Flecknoe.[5] Moreover, one of Butler's own notes to the first part of the poem (1:1, ll. 639–40) indicates that he was acquainted with Paul Scarron's French burlesque, *Virgile Travesti,* published in Paris in 1648; and, as William Horne has shown, Butler would have been familiar with the metaphoric motifs (particularly the "Rump joke") and the prototypical figure of abuse (the "stout Colonel") common to the Royalist burlesque poems collected in an anthology called *Rump,* published in 1662.[6]

Attempts to measure the extent of Butler's borrowings from Rabelais, Cervantes, or Spenser tell us little, however, about the origin of *Hudibras* or its meaning.[7] A more useful sense of that relationship is suggested by Michael Seidel's metaphor of "satiric inheritance," which includes not only general family resemblances, but the discontinuance and degeneration of inheritable traits in both content and form. In Seidel's "generative" (or, more accurately, *degenerative*) sense, *Don Quixote* is itself an example of "revisionary inheritance," and *Hudibras,* Seidel claims, is "a further revision of the quixotic revision of the chivalric mission."[8] Although *Don Quixote* and *Hudibras* both submit their heroes to "an extravagant chivalric prototype revised by a satirically contingent fable," of which the former is designed to lead the hero out of his extravagance, the latter is designed to abandon him in it.[9] *Don Quixote,* and *Gargantua and Pantagruel* as well, may also be said to have passed on to *Hudibras* a "carnival sense of the world" and, in their preservation of a body of traditional festive imagery and a principle of generic destabilization, the model of what Mikhail Bakhtin called the "carnivalesque."[10] Spenser, Seidel interestingly points out, passed on to Butler the model for an "internecine romance," a story of civil war, schism, and the breakdown of the state-as-family. The three sisters (Perissa, Medina, and Elissa, the personifications of excess, moderation, and lack), and their respective lovers (Sans-loy, Guyon, and Huddibras) create a discord which is finally resolved by sovereign power (Gloriana and King Arthur). That power is, of course, absent in the Commonwealth context of *Hudibras,* which takes the model of discord but not of resolution as its satiric inheritance from Spenser.[11]

It is remarkable that Butler's letter to Sir George Oxenden makes no mention of any literary analogue of *Hudibras* and instead equates the poem (i.e., the published "First Part") with its putative "real-life" models. Butler there all but denies the literariness of *Hudibras,* precluding further interpretation and claiming for himself credit only for a sort of painterly skill at rendering and then returning that credit back upon the "pleasant" humor of the model who inspired it. Even Butler's "chiefe designe" ("a just Acco$^t$ of y$^e$ Ridiculous folly & Knavery of y$^e$ Presbyterian & Independent Factions") was manifest in this *real* material: by focusing upon the particular (the "perpetual disputes" between the knight and his clerk, "as you will find up & downe in y$^e$ Booke"), he produced a general picture of the uneasy alliance of Presbyterians and Independents within the party of Puritans, a situation that existed from the end of 1647 to the end of 1648, when Colonel Pride finally purged Parliament of its Presbyterian members. Historically, as in Butler's poem, the differences between these religious viewpoints arose over questions of church government.

The Presbyterian scheme of ecclesiastical reform replaced the rule of bishops in the Anglican Church with a complex hierarchy of authority, a system in which individual congregations were governed by Presbyters, a number of congregations by a Classical Assembly or Classis, the Classes by a Provincial Synod, and the entire structure by a National Synod. The Independents, on the other hand, tolerated no authority over individual congregations; and, as expressed by Ralpho in the first canto of the poem, they regarded the terms "*Provincial, Classick, National* as Mere humane Creature-cobwebs all" (1:1, ll. 807–8), and as no more lawful than a bearbaiting, which a Puritan parliament had declared illegal in 1642. The Independent derived his authority from a "liberty of conscience" and from a private "light" that guided him in matters of religion; and these assumptions the more conservative Presbyterians regarded as a license for dangerous innovation. Relations between Presbyterians and Independents were also strained by the fact that the Independents became a powerful force in Cromwell's army and that by 1647 they had gained political ascendency over the Presbyterians there. Butler alludes to this power shift in the scene in which Hudibras, after trying to force Ralpho to serve as his proxy in a whipping, is warned by his squire to remember "how in *Arms* and *Politicks*" the Independents have triumphed over the "holy Tricks" of Hudibras's party:

> *Trepan'd* your Party with *Intregue,*
> And took your *Grandees* down a peg.
> *New-modell'd* th' *Army,* and *Cashir'd*
> All that to *Legion-SMEC* adher'd,
> Made a mere Utensill o' your *Church*
> And after left it in the lurch
> A Scaffold to build up our own,
> And when w' had done with't pul'd it down.
>                          (2:2, ll. 519–28)

Hudibras is the embodiment of both hypocrisy and Presbyterianism in the poem, and because Butler habitually subsumes the second of these labels in the first, it is virtually impossible to define the character of the knight. But the knight comes into somewhat sharper focus when he is placed alongside his Independent companion; we see then that the Presbyterian is, in Butler's sense of the phrase, an ignorant fool. He is encumbered with the commonplaces of learning, the formal apparatus of logic and rhetoric, and the outmoded rituals of religion and knight-

hood. Ralpho, the Independent, is a knave, a realist able to penetrate
rational deception and to deceive others with his own reason. Like his
Independent prototype, the squire is a better fighter and, though he
pretends to be a mystic, a more skillful reasoner than the Presbyterian
knight. In battle, the squire's superiority lies in his practical knowledge of when to press an advantage and when to retreat; and, in an
argument, he gets the better of Hudibras first by attacking the reality
of words and then by arguing that words are the best weapons of war.
This apparent inconsistency is not merely an expression of Butler's
ambivalent attitude toward reason,[12] but also stands as an effective
representation of the unprincipled opportunism of the Independent and
his party. We might notice in this connection Butler's prose reflection
about the relationship between Don Quixote and Sancho Panza:
". . . the Author of Don Quixot, makes Sancho (though a Natural
Fool) much more wise and Politique then his Master with all his
Study'd, and acquir'd Abilities" (57:2).
    Although it is impossible to say whether Butler expected the charac-
ters and actions of his poem to bear any additional allegorical significance than that mentioned in his letter to Oxenden, few readers have
been able to resist extending this function in their interpretations of the
poem. Even in Butler's own day, as he indicated in the letter,
". . . some curious witts heere pretend to discouer ceartaine Psons of
Quality w$^{th}$ whome they say those Characters agree, but since I doe not
know who they are I cannot tell you till I see theire Commentaries but
am content (since I cannot helpe it) y$^t$ every man should make what
applications he pleases of it, either to himselfe or others." Many of these
discoveries or identifications were to appear in an "Alphabetical Key to
Hudibras," which has been ascribed to Sir Roger L'Estrange (1616–
1704); though the "Key" first appeared in the Posthumous Works (1715),
Zachary Grey claimed that L'Estrange was personally acquainted with
Butler and "undoubtedly received the Secret from him."[13] Specifically,
the "Key" attempts to supply the historical originals of Butler's characters: Hudibras is Sir Samuel Luke; Ralph, Isaac Robinson, "a zealous
Botcher in Moorfields, who . . . was always contriving some new
Quirpocut of Church-Government"; Crowdero, "one Jackson a Milliner
in the New-Exchange," who took up fiddle playing in taverns after
losing a leg in the service of the Roundheads; and the widow is "the
precious Relique of Aminadab Wilmot, an Independent, kill'd at the
Fight of Edgehill; and having Two-hundred Pounds per Annum left her
for a Jointure." Some indication of the questionable authority of this

"Key" may be gathered from the liklihood that its characterization of Ralph/Isaac Robinson was drawn not from life, but from "a fanciful creation" included in John Cleveland's *Character of a London Diurnall* (1645).[14]

In 1923, Hardin Craig traced the "dim outlines of a political allegory" in part 1 of *Hudibras,* stating that "the brave resistance of the bear, his flight, and establishment in a place of at least temporary comfort" suggest "the flight of King Charles from Hampton Court to Carisbrook," and that the knight's defeat by the bearbaiters suggests "the defeat of the Presbyterians and their overthrow by the leaders of the army."[15] Though it naturally follows from such an interpretation that Bruin, the bear in the poem, stands for Charles (and, with a bit more interpretive pressure, that the butcher Talgol stands for the Puritan commander Thomas Fairfax, and the "hard hostler" Colon for Cromwell), Craig, whose primary interest was dating the composition of the poem, did not insist upon such identifications.

For W. S. Miller, however, the allegory of *Hudibras* is far too detailed for Butler to have been unaware of what he was accomplishing. Miller not only finds Butler's anti-Puritan sentiments objectified in Hudibras and Ralpho, but also uncovers vestiges of the poet's supposed pre-Restoration anti-Royalism in the poem. "It is not unlikely," he writes, "that *Hudibras* took shape . . . from ambivalent feelings—anti-Presbyterian and anti-Independent, but nevertheless incorporating symbolic values for the king and for Cavalier forces that the Restoration would not tolerate."[16] If, as Miller assumes, part 1 was taking shape in the 1640s, when Butler, he further assumes, was feeling little sympathy with a king "who had often flouted the British constitution," then, he concludes, Talgol, Bruin, Trulla, and Magnano "certainly" appear as "Royalist symbols of some sort." Rather than recast these characters as Puritans after Charles's restoration, Butler merely strengthened "the anti-Puritan exterior" of the poem, taking refuge in the obscurity that "he was quite capable of achieving without the will to do so."[17] The immense success of *Hudibras* in the Restoration rested, then, upon a misinterpretation of the poem—one that Mr. Miller would have us believe Butler himself could have sanctioned, if not willed.

Actually, the temporal dimensions of *Hudibras* are even more complex than Miller believes. As John Wilders has shown, there are three demonstrable time levels in the poem: one "on which the characters look back in retrospect" (from 1640 to 1647); a second "in which Butler visualized the action of his poem as taking place" (between the end of 1647 and the end of 1648); and a third "during which he actually wrote" the major portion of part 1 (between December 1653 and September 1658).[18] Nevertheless, Miller's hypothesis of an equally complex allegory in the poem is unconvincing. Butler's pre-Restoration parliamentary sympathies rely principally on an assumption: "Butler's association with John Selden at Wrest would certainly seem to have guaranteed Butler's alignment with the parliamentary cause."[19] Now it is quite reasonable to assume that the distinguished John Selden would have exerted considerable influence upon the young Butler, but there can be no *certain guarantee* as to its precise nature. However, we do know that Butler's earliest poetic efforts—"Upon the Parliament which Deliberated about Making Oliver King" and "A Ballad"—are anything but soft on Parliament. On the other hand, Butler's supposed post-Restoration concern about not being on the right side is belied by a poem like the "Satyr upon the Licentious Age of Charles the 2d."

It is true that the imaginary world of *Hudibras* seems frequently about to verge upon the historical outlines of the real world of Commonwealth England. We should consider, for example, the political overtones in Butler's explanation of how Crowdero, the fiddler, lost his leg (an allusion to a Staffordshire folk tradition of crowning a king of musicians): "He bravely vent'ring at a Crown, / By chance of War was beaten down" (1:2, ll. 139–40). Or we have the passage describing Hudibras's riding out upon his first adventure:

> So have I seen with armed heel,
> A Wight bestride a *Common-weal;*
> While still the more he kick'd and spurr'd,
> The less the sullen Jade has stirr'd.
>                                    (1:1, ll. 917–20)

And, in this connection, we might notice that Miller's citation of lines from a contemporary ballad on the Long Parliament is both apposite and enlightening:

> Will you buy the Rumps great saddle,
> With which it jockey'd the nation?
> And here is the bit and the bridle,
> And curb of Dissimulation . . .[20]

Lines in the portrait of the astrologer Sidrophel call to mind the features of William Lilly and Sir Paul Neile; and Hudibras's wooing of the widow suggests the attempts of the Puritans to become the lords of "Dame Religion," of England herself, or—in view of the fact that she exposes Hudibras's lies—as the personification of Right Reason or Truth. And yet Earl Miner (whose suggestion I have cited last here) remarks that the widow "must be taken primarily as a widow and as a woman," "that Butler's allegory or allusions do not permit us to identify historical events in his major episodes."[21]

Beside these passages of oblique suggestiveness, we must place others that impose upon the world of the poem direct references to the real world—negating thereby the reason for allegory. If Hudibras's battle with the bearbaiters was meant to represent English politics in the 1640s, why then should Butler have bothered to summarize explicitly the Puritan struggles of the same period in the knight's harangue to the rabble (1:2, ll. 493–682)? Or, if Hudibras's attempt to break his vow to the widow in part 2 represents allegorically the duplicity of the Puritan movement in England, why then is the point made again directly, as in the following?

> Did not our *Worthies* of the *House,*
> Before they broke the *Peace,* break *Vows?*
> For having free'd us, first from both
> Th' *Allegeance,* and *Supremacy-Oath;*
> Did they not, next, compel the *Nation,*
> To take, and break the *Protestation?*
> (2:2, ll. 149–54)

Such passages suggest that the historical allegory in *Hudibras* is at best sporadic and improvisational, like the more local effects of wit in the poem. When his satiric invention suggested the features of reality, Butler eagerly seized upon and developed the resemblance; but his invention was not determined by the data of history, nor would he invent a witty resemblance to such data merely for its own sake. Resemblances of the first sort reveal and intensify identity, illuminating and enlivening the literary image with recognitions of reality; allegory of the second sort—"continued Allegory, or darke conceit," as Spenser identified it—conceals identity, either deliberately, or by making the act of recognition a gratuitous intellectual exercise.

I pointed out in the preceding chapter Butler's interest in metaphor and allegory as a means of deceiving men for their own good; but he clearly disapproved of the use of allegory for such purposes of conceal- ment as Miller attributes to *Hudibras*. "Allegories are only usefull," Butler observed in the prose observations, "when they serve as In- stances, to illustrate Some obscure Truth": "But when a Truth, Plaine enough, is forced to Serve an Allegory, it is a praeposterous mistake of the End of it; which is to make obscure things Plaine, not Plaine things obscure . . . beside the Preposterous Difficulty of forcing things against their Naturall inclinations, which at the best do's but discover how much wit a man may have to no purpose; there being no such Argument of a slight minde as an elaborate Triffle" (126:5). Readers, it seems, tend to regard all satire as obscurantist, "darke," as if the "truth" of allegory—like that discovered by the virtuosos in "The Ele- phant in the Moon"—were by definition particular and therefore hid- den in order to be disclosed. Butler, however, observed that although wit might be prompted by individuals, it performs its true function when it sheds light on general human nature; for "wit is like Science not of Particulars, but universals," and "Arguments drawn from Par- ticulars signify little to universal Nature, which is the Proper object of Science" (13:2).

## Satire

In view of this criticism of allegory as a "darke conceit," Butler would seem less likely to write such an "elaborate Triffle" himself than to parody it or to ridicule the type of mind that produces it. This is not to say that *Hudibras* is a parody of the allegorical mode—although a passage like that in which Ralpho proves that "*Synods* are mystical *Bear- gardens*" (1:2, ll. 1095–1250) has been read by Paul Korshin as a satire of typological exegesis.[22] But, in another way, the poem is much concerned with trifles and with those who elaborate upon them. Two examples immediately come to mind: first, the moral scruple of the pharisaical Puritan whose conscience, Butler wrote in the Character of "A Hypocritical Nonconformist," is so "taken up with such slight and little Matters, that it is impossible, it should ever be at Leisure to consider Things of greater Weight and Importance" (47); and, second, the ceremonious conventions celebrated in heroic romance, the branch of literature which, Butler noted, "handle's the slightest, and most Impertinent Follys in the world in a formall Serious and unnaturall way" (13:3).

For Butler, however, chivalric punctilio and Puritan casuistry were merely symptoms of a far more pervasive human tendency—of "that primal energy," as Alvin Kernan defines it, "which drives the world toward the strange grotesque shapes it assumes" in all satire.[23] Kernan reminds us that great satire conceives of folly and vice in positive rather than in negative terms—more, that is, as an active presence or force than as an absence or loss of value. "The better authors of satire," writes Kernan, "have been literary Manichees who have shown an ancient and powerful force operating constantly and expressing its own nature through all lands and times."[24] "Dullness," that great, weighty, and dark source of all uncreative and destructive energy in Pope's *Dunciad,* admirably illustrates the idea; for Pope's word is "broad enough to cover the wide range of idiocy and viciousness portrayed in all satire."[25]

Butler also employs the word "dullness" in Pope's sense of a laborious activity or drudgery, but more frequently his name for this potential is "ignorance." Like dullness, ignorance is a precipitate and increasing force or weight, the impulse of a motion. As described in the Character of an "Ignorant Man," "dull ignorance has the same operation with the wiser part of the world as lead has in the test of metals, that being apply'd to gold carries away all the baser metals that are mixt with it . . ." (282). As a source of energy, it is, like zeal or enthusiasm, a dehumanizing power that turns its possessor into a mere machine; Butler's Character the "Fanatic," an early sketch of Swift's "Mechanical operation of the spirit," describes a "Puppet Saint, that moves he knows not how, and his Ignorance is the dull leaden Weight that puts all his Parts in Motion" (128).

Though conventionally the word "ignorance" implies an absence (and of course it is caused by the want of knowledge, particularly self-knowledge), Butler's examples of ignorance are distinguished by excess rather than inadequacy—to be precise, by their efforts to disguise and overcompensate for their shortcomings; for Butler, then, intense energy, unattached to intelligence, is the primary characteristic of ignorance. As he noted in the prose observations, under the heading "Learning and Knowledge," nature "relieves the Necessities of those, who are ashamd to have them known to others" by

perswading them they injoy that which of all things they are the most destitute of. And hence it come's that no men are so indefatigable Drudges in all manner of Sciences, as those to whom Nature ha's allow'd the weakest abilities to attaine to any perfection in them: for Dunces are commonly observd to be the hardest Students, as those always prove the most passionate Lovers, that meet with the most Coy and disdainfull Mistresses. (20)

In business, the energies of ignorance emerge in the bureaucratic passion for red tape; in society, they appear as a preoccupation with clothes and manners; in education, as an academic interest in form and method rather than in substance; and in government, as a concern for the letter rather than the spirit of the law. Wherever stupidity, ineptness, and moral flaccidity use words, acts, or attentions to make the simple and plain difficult and obscure, the trivial seem significant, the low high—there, Butler suggests, we are confronted with ignorance.

*Hudibras* is a satire of ignorance in this sense of the word. Butler's hero is introduced to us as both a "domestick" knight (a justice of the peace) and a knight "errant": he is "Great on the Bench, Great in the Saddle" (1:1, l. 23). In the Knight's first words in the poem, spoken to his squire as they set out upon adventure, Hudibras says:

> We that are wisely mounted higher
> Then Constables, in Curule wit,
> When on Tribunal bench we sit,
> Like Speculators, should forsee,
> From *Pharos* of Authority,
> Portended Mischiefs farther then
> Low Proletarian Tithing-men.
>                           (1:1, ll. 708–14)

The saddle, a surrogate tribunal bench, is, like the "oratorial machines" in Swift's *Tale of a Tub,* a means of achieving altitude, of being seen; it is also the burlesque seat of the far-seeing providential hero, although for Hudibras seeing "farther" is not only *fore*seeing but also *over*seeing or magnifying "Portended Mischiefs." This tendency to make much of little, to turn a bearbaiting into a Jesuit plot against Puritan solidarity, or a skimmington into a dangerous pagan rite, is the form in which Hudibras's ignorance reveals itself. The knight's fondness for pedantic language and Puritan cant ("hard words," as the poem refers to it)[26] is another example of this tendency, for language is the primary means by which men invest insignificance with importance. "Some occult design doth ly / In bloudy *Cynarctomachy,*" the knight at one point informs his squire, and "sure some mischief will come of it: / Unless . . . we averruncate it" (1:1, ll. 745–46; 750–52). And Butler comments in a note to these lines that "Cynarctomachy signifies nothing in the World, but a Fight between *Dogs* and *Bears,* though both the Learned and Ignorant agree, that in such words very great Knowledge is contained: and our Knight as one, or both of those, was of the same opinion." Butler adds, in explanation of "averruncate": "Another of the same kind, which though it appear ever so Learned, and Profound, means nothing else but the weeding of Corn."

In religious matters, the energy of ignorance appears as an exquisite sensitivity (a "strict tenderness") to the slightest doctrinal difference or offense. Butler observed in his notebook that "zeal is of no use without Opposition and Conscience has no way to shew its Tendernesse, but in seeking Occasion to take offence at some thing or other, and the more slight, and triviall the better, for it's strict tendernes, and Innocence appeares to be the greater, and the world will not be apt to suspect the Fayth and Integrity of those, that are severe and scrupulous in small matters" (34:3). Thus, in men of a spiritual or intellectual calling (in men like Sir Hudibras), ignorance is a conjuring as well as a magnifying power—able, that is, to create appearances of the internal qualities such men lack; it becomes, in other words, simple pretense, hypocrisy, a serious sort of play with the relations between signs and things. By turning the everyday concerns of men into critical questions of honor or conscience and then magnifying them in words and actions, Hudibras appears to be all mind and spirit—all "inner man." His insistence that "th'Immortal Intellect / . . . / Is free from outward bruise or maim, / Which nought external can expose / To gross material bangs or blows" (2:1, ll. 191–96) is meant to convey his contempt for the material security and physical safety of the "outer man."

But, of course, Hudibras is nothing *but* "outer man," and he cannot ignore its demands: his bruises ache, his stomach growls, and his nose is assaulted by the fecal smells of his own fear. His spiritual pretensions, likened in the following lines to one of the great moments in heroic literature, are vain illusions; the knight's paunch and rump are his only real burdens:

> . . . as *Aeneas* bore his Sire
> Upon his shoulders through the fire:
> Our Knight did bear no less a Pack
> Of his own Buttocks on his back:
> Which now had almost got the upper-
> Hand of his Head, for want of Crupper.

> To poise this equally, he bore
> A *Paunch* of the same bulk before:
> Which still he had a speciall care
> To keep well cramm'd with thrifty fare;
> As White-pot, Butter-milk, and Curds.
>                                    (1:1, ll. 287–97)

Read as irony, then, the outward signs of Hudibras's nit-picking attention to matters of heroism, honor, love, and conscience signify the
absence of these concerns in the knight; moral *sound*-ness (Butler puns
on the word) is merely a Puritan vocal mannerism, the "sound and
*twang of Nose*" (1:3, ll. 1157–58); conscience is a garment whose
"*Wear-and-tear*" may be "patch'd-up and turn'd" (3:1, ll. 1182–83).
But the Puritan hypocrite was, for Butler, not only one who out-
wardly manifested the signifiers of what he inwardly lacked, a simple
inversion of the sign of *Quixotism,* in which real inner qualities go
without signifiers. In one respect at least, Hudibras is exactly what he
appears to be: a fat man, driven by excessive appetites—a belly
"cramm'd with . . . White-pot, Buttermilk, and Curds" (1:1, l.
297)—the trademark of Sancho Panza, not Quixote. As Linda Troost
observes, "to deflate the hypocritical Puritans, Butler shows their contradictory behavior on the most fundamental and universal level: nour-
ishment."[27] Puritan hypocrisy, in other words, not only creates the
appearance of what is absent; it also hides what is actually present.
Butler catches its contradictory nature in the phrase "Spiritual Carnevall" (213:3), his point being that the physical energies and appetites of
hyprocrites and zealots are so great that the diversionary spectacle of
traditional carnival indulgence can no longer contain them and must
become instead a spectacle of concealment and denial: "that extraordinary and supercilious Reservdnes which he [the hypocrite] always puts
on in Publique, is not to conceal nothing," Butler observed, "but hide
something that is worse" (213:3). As we shall later see, Hudibras is the
combination of Cervantes's man of spirit and man of flesh, the walking
emblem of hypocrisy.
   The comic conception of self-betraying hypocrisy and self-defeating
ignorance underlies the form of *Hudibras,* the nature of which, according to Richmond P. Bond, is "so complex in its origin and purpose and
method that it defies final classification."[28] Bond is speaking of the
classification of Butler's poem as a species of burlesque, the general
class to which he nevertheless provisionally assigns it under the name

"Hudibrastic," a species of "low burlesque" which places subject above style, and degrades a general (as travesty degrades a particular) literary model by means of an undignified treatment.[29] (Bond contrasts Hudibrastic burlesque and travesty with the "high burlesque" mock-poem and parody, forms which place style above subject, and borrow respectively a general or specific literary manner to convey the unworthy subject. But Bond is the first to admit that his tidy paradigm of burlesque forms provides inadequate space for Butler's poem. Though *Hudibras* treats a subject of some degree of seriousness, and though its manner is obviously coarse, its hero is not, for one thing, sufficiently elevated to permit that stylistic denigration that characterizes low burlesque. On the other hand, the process of degrading the hero is not caused solely by rhetorical contrast, as is normally the case in high burlesque. Bond admits that Hudibras is "neither a trivial nor a dignified personage" as he is given to the reader and that Butler both "caricatures" the knight "and also places him in an heroic framework." As a result, Bond finds the procedure of the poem "antithetical and dangerous," and its technique "confusing."[30]

Bond is not alone in remarking about the confusing nature of the poem. James Sutherland has observed that "*Hudibras* contains burlesque elements, but is not itself a burlesque poem";[31] and John Wilders assigns to it the antithetical functions of both the mock-heroic and the Hudibrastic burlesque. At times, he says, its literary allusions "emphasize the meanness of the characters in comparison with their epic trappings. . . . But the antithesis between form and subject also acts in the opposite direction, the presence of coarse characters and 'low' actions within a heroic framework reflecting critically upon the literary conventions themselves."[32] Edward Ames Richards urges us to ignore Bond's related species of parody, travesty, mock-heroic and Hudibrastic burlesque as a "confusing field of esthetic relativities" and suggests, instead, that we regard *Hudibras* as a "burlesque" in the simplest sense of that term—as a "variation or distortion."[33] And Ruth Nevo, who sees the poem at "the heart and center of the [burlesque] mode in its historical seventeenth century sense," nevertheless observes that a contemporary like Dryden exempted Butler from his general condemnation of the form.[34] Clearly, Bond did not exaggerate in observing that "the greatest obstacle to consistent nomenclature in this area has been the nature of Butler's poem."

Two other critical accounts of *Hudibras,* however, have managed to avoid these difficulties of classification. Ian Jack, for one, removes the poem altogether from the category of burlesque (in Bond's sense); in maintaining that "the characteristic mode of satire in *Hudibras* is the opposite of the mock-heroic," he means that it is simply "low satire." Butler's method, Jack argues, "is that of straightforward 'diminution' "; his subject is "as different as possible from that of the romantic epic poet . . . and his style is equally remote from that of heroic verse. . . . The essence of low satire could not be more simple."[35] Ultimately, we may agree: *everything* in *Hudibras* is diminished or debased. But whatever is debased must first of all have been elevated, and Jack's view of *Hudibras* as "low satire" fails, I believe, to take account of the elevated materials in the poem—if only as matter for eventual debasement. Compare with the passage from *Hudibras* quoted several paragraphs earlier (1:1, ll. 287–97), that which associates the distinctly low description of the knight's burden (paunch and rump) with the burden of Aeneas (Anchises), the opening, mock-heroic lines of Dryden's *Mac Flecknoe*

> All things are subject to decay,
> And when Fate summons, monarchs must obey.
> This Flecknoe found

and we see that Butler, just as much as Dryden, makes us—at least initially—think of the differences between the terms in these two statements. This is not to discount Jack's distinction between mock-heroic and "low satire"; on the contrary, I wish to emphasize it by noticing that Dryden's lines leave the standard of dignity intact while Butler's undermine it. Butler, in other words, introduces the heroic into the poem as both an instrument of debasement and as matter to be debased.

David Farley-Hills, from a different critical perspective, redefines "burlesque" in order to include *Hudibras,* but exclude mock-heroic and satire in general. If satire destroys things because "they are seen to be bad" according to supposed standards, burlesque, he contends, destroys them "for the fun of destruction." What makes *Hudibras* burlesque rather than satire, according to Farley-Hills, "is the exuberant comedy and the lack of consistent viewpoint."[36] Whereas the mock-hero's pretensions to dignity define a set of values that mock him, the values claimed by Hudibras are themselves mocked by the poet, indicting the hero only insofar as they are themselves made to appear shabby; the poem's effect on the reader, therefore, "is to confuse and ultimately destroy the world that it seeks to create." Hudibras, then, is "both cowardly knave and clown hero."[37] Such a view seems especially appropriate in a discussion of *Hudibras,* which characteristically sets forth incongruities (between the ideal and the real, the high and the low) only to reduce both elements to a common level of absurdity. We might consider this method to be that of an antipoet, of one who has lost faith in the ethical norms of his age and in the moral efficacy of traditional poetic means. *Hudibras* was written in a time of cultural decay, not only the aftermath of a reigning Puritan ideology, but a time when the ascendant values of a "Restored" monarchy appeared—at least for Butler—to be a dying myth. Butler's burlesque destructiveness, therefore, extends even to the conventions of learning and heroism (for example, the scholastic hairsplitting and legal wrangling of the knight and squire, the invocation to the muse of Withers and Prynne, and the mock-catalogue of bearbaiters). Such conventions exist as mere empty forms in *Hudibras.*

Butler's doggerel measure is an even more pervasive illustration of this attitude. "People expect a 'marked rhythm' to imply something worth marking," Walter Bagehot observed; "they are displeased at the visible waste of a powerful instrument. . . . The burst of metre . . . incident to high imagination, should not be wasted on petty matters which prose does as well. . . ."[38] Hudibrastic octosyllabics deliberately violate this principle for comic effect, metrically inciting an expectation of significance which is subsequently left unsatisfied. Beneath their slapdash carelessness there is an unforgiving metricality to Butler's lines that he made more and more obvious in his revisions of the poem. Notice his tinkering with the spelling *squire* / *squier* (monosyllable / disyllable), carelessly transposed in the first printing of a couplet, but put metrically right in the second: "Never did trusty Squire with Knight, / Or Knight with Squier jump more right" (1:1, ll. 619–20). Butler used the conventions of poetry metalinguistically—not, that is, as tools to be used to organize materials into a poem, but as a means to signifying the concept of poeticality. They certify, sarcastically, that this is *"the Stamp and Coyne"* of poetry: see and hear how it answers for *"the Allay, and want of Intrinsic value"* (138:1)!

The metricality of the Hudibrastic line also exploits the phonetic value of words at the expense of their semantic value. As we are told at the beginning of part 2: "those that write in *Rhime,* still make / The one *Verse,* for the others sake" (2:1, ll. 27–28). The insistence of Butler's doggerel meter and doggerel rhyme acts as a powerful weapon, capable of synthesizing, truncating, and fracturing words, irrespective of their meanings:

> And Pulpit, Drum Ecclesiastick,
> Was beat with fist, instead of a stick;
> (1:1, ll. 11–12)

> There was an ancient sage *Philosopher,*
> That had read *Alexander Ross* over;
> (1:2, ll. 1–2)

> Us'd him so like a base *Rascallion,*
> That old *Pyg-* (what d'y' call him?) malion.
> (1:3, ll. 327–28)

Verse that can thus reduce language to mere sound provides the perfect vehicle for the expression of a system of debased values. A similar speciousness exists in many of the metaphors in the poem. Ruth Nevo has termed these "burlesque similitudes," their principle residing in "a concertina-like expansion and contraction of dimensions." There may, she says, "be a disparity between the quantitative treatment and the triviality of the thing treated; or between the magnitude of the simile's vehicle and the littleness of its tenor; or vice versa. . . ."[39] Butler's figures are only formally metaphorical, however; they might also be described, therefore, as examples of what the next century will call "false wit." And I might note here that, although Addison himself appreciated that Butler was ridiculing false wit in lines like those just quoted, he objected to the public's fondness for Hudibrastic wit for its own sake.[40]

Paradoxically, what we respond to in such structures is, finally, not incongruity, but a congruity which is false because purely formal. Why do the final two syllables of "Ecclesiastic" and the phrase "a stick" make a comic rhyme? Because we are forced to read the second as a perfect echo of the first, that is, as a meaningless tautology. And the double rhymes of the poem exaggerate this effect by claiming an even more extensive identity in the lines. If Butler's figures are burlesque, then, it is because they surrender the function of true wit (the making of truth intelligible, as Butler defined it) in order to become self-destructive puns; resemblances and congruities of sounds or syllables—not ideas—are wittily used to reveal their own falseness. In effect, they function precisely as Butler's hero does and as the heroic and learned elements function in the larger structure of the poem.

As burlesque, *Hudibras* resembles nothing so much as the heroic poem likely to result from Alexander Pope's mock-recipe for writing one found in *The Art of Sinking in Poetry:* first, "depress what is High"; second, "raise what is Base and Low to a ridiculous Visibility." "When both these can be done at once, then is the *Bathos* in Perfection; as when a Man is set with his Head downward, and his Breech upright, his Degredation is compleat: one End of him is as high as ever, only that End is the Wrong one."[41] Alvin Kernan has observed that Pope was dealing here with the satirist's difficulty of showing "that the mad world he constructs is truly mad, that it is the breech which is up, not the head."[42]

This is no problem in the carnivalized world of *Hudibras,* where heroic conventions are debased as casually as pretense and failure appear to be licensed; where, it seems, "anything goes," and one may argue, for instance, that "*Beards,* the nearer that they tend / To th'*Earth,* still grow more reverend: / And *Cannons* shoot the higher pitches, / The lower we let down their breeches" (2:1, ll. 261–64). But burlesque and carnival do not, contrary to Farley-Hills's view, preclude satire; in fact, it might be argued that *Hudibras* presents the carnival sense of the world only because of its affinity with that variety of satire called *Menippean,* which Mikhail Bakhtin regards as "one of the main carriers" of the carnival spirit into modern literature.[43] Menippean satire tends to be expressed in prose rather than in verse (though it often contains passages of verse); it is narrative rather than declamation, a mishmash of genres rather than unified discourse; it is also journalistic in its concern with current affairs and topical issues, though, as Bakhtin says, it is "free of legend and not fettered by any demands for an external verisimilitude to life."[44] On *Hudibras*'s conformity to these characteristics, earlier opinions have differed, the agreed upon correspondences being largely formal—the poem's interpolation of letters, for instance, or the debate between the Presbyterian and Independent statesmen in the second canto of part 3.[45] More to the point, however, is Bakhtin's conviction that Menippean satire's "willful narrative mixing of high and low, of sublime and bathetic,"[46] its medley of inserted genres and of the languages of the church, the courtroom, and the marketplace reveal the monological nature of presumed truths. As Craig Howes puts it, "placing a privileged language back within this chorus . . . exposes individual truth to the glare of the cultural moment."[47]

## Plot

Although Butler's rejection of the standards by which satire normally judges human behavior has created special problems for critics attempting to define the formal nature of *Hudibras,* readers have encountered little difficulty in understanding the general satiric intention of the poem. Just as Butler's irreverent attitude toward the conventions of poetry and romance is unmistakably conveyed in the materials of the poem, so there can be no uncertainty that Sir Hudibras is given to us as an ignorant fool, as, that is, a character who indicts himself by his own actions. The plot of the poem itself makes us aware of the nature of ignorance.

Though the "story" which Butler received from his fellow lodger in Holbourne provided the general outline of only part 1 of *Hudibras,* the central idea of part 2 and its part 3 sequel may be seen as a natural outgrowth of the poet's original satiric impulse. That impulse, as I have already suggested, was the exposure of the falseness of the heroic view of life—a pattern of lies and pretenses that was formally embodied in romance and actively practiced, Butler suggests, by the Puritans. Parts 1 and 2 of *Hudibras*—the ultimate victory of the fiddler over the knight and the knight's unsuccessful suit of a widow—comprise, then, the conventional matter of romance: "for what else / Is in [romance]," Butler observed, "but *Love* and *Battles?*" (1:2, ll. 5–6). Accordingly, the narrative unity of all three parts of the poem is "heroic"—or some more or less consistent treatment of heroic materials.

Part 1, "th' Adventure of the *Bear* and *Fiddle,*" is the story of the knight's temporary victory and ultimate defeat at the hands of a group of bearbaiters. The "heroic" action of the episode is taken up with two battles. In the first, in canto 2, Hudibras and Ralph manage, largely by accident, to stop a bearbaiting by dispersing its promoters and spectators and then by arresting and confining in the stocks its central figure, a fiddler named Crowdero; in the second battle, reported in canto 3, Hudibras and Ralph are themselves defeated and confined in the stocks, in the first of a series of comic reversals of romance conventions. The transition between these two battles is also presented in two scenes: the first of these (1:3, ll. 25–292) describes the routed bearbaiters as they regroup for a concerted attack upon the knight and his squire; the second (1:3, ll. 297–412) depicts the lucky warrior as an unlucky lover. Hudibras is a rejected suitor who—having "resolv'd . . . either to renounce [his lady] quite, / Or for a while play least in sight" (1:3, ll.

366–68)—nevertheless believes that his premature victory in canto 2 "might work upon her" (1:3, l. 378):

> So from his Couch the *Knight* did start,
> To seize upon the Widow's heart;
> Crying with hasty tone and hoarse,
> *Ralpho,* dispatch, To horse, to horse.
>                                  (1:3, ll. 409–12)

The accidental encounter which follows is of course pure farce—the collision of the panting lover and the angry bearbaiters—but this confrontation also seems designed to challenge the orthodox critical assumption that love is a suitable subject in heroic literature. Butler later calls attention to this implicit criticism at the beginning of part 2 where, after announcing that he will "observe *Romantique* Method" by exchanging "rusty Steel" with "Love's more gentle stile" (2:1, ll. 1–5), he pretends to defend his decision in an ironic note to these lines: "The beginning of this Second Part may perhaps seem strange and abrupt to those who do not know, that it was written of purpose, in imitation of *Virgil,* who begins the IV Book of his *Aeneides* in the very same manner. . . . And this is enough to satisfy the curiosity of those who believe that Invention and Fancy ought to be measur'd (like Cases in Law) by Precedents, or else they are in the power of the Critique" (100).

The reference in part 1 to the knight's love for the widow is not, then, a hastily contrived link between the two parts of the poem; instead, his love is an important element of its *"Romantique* Method." Butler must fairly soon have recognized the limits of his initial ridicule of chivalric military exploits, the physical, external absurdities of the knight-errant. But love, or the pretense of love, reveals the internal workings of his hero, the complex casuistry and knavery that were Butler's chief interests in the study of human behavior. The more damaging moral exposure of the knight in part 2 represents, then, not a change in the poet's conception of his hero[48] but rather an extension of his original satiric purpose to another dimension of the hero's character. Moreover, Hudibras's interest in the widow becomes the crucial motive of subsequent action in the poem. It impels the hero toward his defeat in the second battle and his subsequent humiliation in the stocks, and it spurs his efforts in part 2 to regain his former standing as a knight.

This development of the action begins with the widow's arrival at the place of the knight's confinement, a reversal of the traditional romantic

rescue of a lady by a knight. Indeed, Hudibras's suffering is reduced to
the unheroic "labor" of an expectant mother awaiting delivery:

> She vow'd she would go see the sight,
> And visit the distressed *Knight,*
> To do the office of a Neighbor,
> And be a *Gossip* at his Labour:
> And from his wooden Jayl the Stocks
> To set at large his Fetter-locks,
> And by Exchange, Parole, or Ransome,
> To free him from th'Inchanted Mansion.
>                                 (2:1, ll. 87–94)

Hudibras's lady departs from her romantic prototype in several other
respects. The disdain of conventional mistresses for their lovers is, in the
widow's case, an outright contempt for Hudibras that is further travestied in her perverse taste of loving "none but only such / As scorn'd and
hated her as much" (1:3, ll. 335–36). Moreover, the unlikely tasks that
she assigns the knight are contrived only to reveal his folly and dishonesty. Thus, in part 2 (1, ll. 825 ff.), the widow offers Hudibras the
opportunity of immediate freedom and future matrimony if he promises
to undergo a whipping, a vow he readily makes but does not honor,
justifying his perjury as an act of party loyalty: "the saints did take and
break the oaths of allegiance and supremacy," Susan Staves reminds us;
"they did 'take and break the Protestation'; they did 'take th' *Engagement,*
and disclaim it'; and they did swear to preserve the House of Lords and
later vote to abolish it."[49] True to his calling, the knight tries to make
Ralpho his proxy for the whipping (2:2, ll. 441 ff.), a compromise the
squire threatens to resist with force. The ensuing quarrel is interrupted
by the appearance of a skimmington—a folk ceremony practiced against
shrewish wives—which the hypocritical Hudibras interprets as a heathen
custom that is disrespectful to "that *Sex* . . . To whom the *Saints* [Puri-
tans] are so beholding" (2:2, ll. 773–74). His harangue to the procession
is countered by a barrage of rotten eggs and an even more odoriferous
substance that turns the knight and squire "in quest of nearest *Ponds*"
(2:2, l. 886). On the strength of his bold attempt to defend feminine
honor, Hudibras resolves to swear that he has undergone the whipping
enjoined by the widow; yet, after his most recent humiliation, even his
self-confidence is shaken, and, fearing "what *danger* might accrue, / If she

should find he *swore* untrue" (2:3, ll. 47–48), he seeks the astrologer Sidrophel to learn "how farr the *Dest'nies* take my part" (2:3, l. 96).

In a sense, then, the widow becomes the satirist's accomplice by directing the actions of the hero and by determining the topics of self-defeating discussion. In the first canto of part 2, the narrator speaks in only 219 lines; the remaining 705 are dialogue, over half of which (366 lines) are given to the widow. In the still more dramatic first canto of part 3, she again has the larger part (477 lines); and, perhaps most significant, she is allowed the last word in the poem in "The Ladies Answer to the Knight." Quite literally, she takes over from the author the job of exposing romantic pretensions. At times, she assumes a mask of naivete, as when she first declines to rescue Hudibras from the stocks:

> . . . for a *Lady* no ways *Errant*
> To free a *Knight,* we have no warrant
> In any Authentical *Romance,*
> Or Classique Author yet of *France:*
> And I'de be loath to have you break
> An Ancient *Custom* for a freak,
> Or *Innovation* introduce
> In place of things of *antique* use.
> (2:1, ll. 785–92)

More often, however, the widow voices Butler's own point of view, as in the following criticism of Hudibras's use of romantic poetry in courtship:

> Hold, hold, Quoth she, no more of this,
> Sir *Knight,* you take your aim amiss;
> For you will find it a hard *Chapter,*
> To catch me with *Poetique Rapture,*
> In which your *Mastery* of *Art*
> Doth shew it self, and not your *Heart:*
> Nor will you raise in mine *combustion,*
> By dint of high *Heroique* fustion:
> Shee that with *Poetry* is won,
> Is but a *Desk* to write upon.
> (2:1, ll. 583–92)

I might note here that Butler's treatment of women is ambiguous. In the prose observations, they are spoken of with almost medieval animosity as latter-day Eves who introduce their men to the lies and cheats of proselytizing priests, and in *Hudibras,* Butler makes a point of saying that Puritan women were the easy tools of Parliament in its appeals for money and plate to maintain the army. Is Butler any more sympathetic in his treatment of the widow and the two other women in the poem, Trulla and the victim of the skimmington? Together, they not only expose the unreality of the idealized woman of romance, but also embody the standard targets of traditional antifeminist satire. Hudibras's lady is cynical and cruel; the wife who appears with her henpecked husband in the skimmington is a recognized shrew; and the character of the "bold *Virago,*" Trulla, is implicit in her name. Much has been made of the fact that the women appear to fare better than the men in *Hudibras,* and I shall return to this surprising aspect of the poem in the next chapter. For the moment, however, let us accept the women's triumph over Hudibras and Ralpho as nothing more than what these men deserve.

"The Second Part" of *Hudibras* concludes with another ironic comment on conventional heroism. At the end of the third canto, we see Hudibras spurring his "lofty Beast" *from* "Danger, Fears, and Foes," beating, by "at least three lengths, the wind" (2:3, ll. 1186–90), thereby reversing the equestrian image which initiated the action of the poem (1:1, ll. 910–20). Earlier in this canto (2:3, ll. 543 ff.), Hudibras quarreled with the astrologer, Sidrophel, accusing him not only of trafficking with the devil, but of stealing his purse and his identity. (The last of these accusations alludes to the spurious second part of *Hudibras* (1663), while the first plays upon the recent debate between Presbyterians and judicial astrologers and their more radical sectarian supporters.[50]) While the knight holds Sidrophel and his assistant at bay, Ralpho is sent to "fetch us / A *Cunstable* to seize the Wretches" (2:3, ll. 1015–16), but before the squire can return, the astrologer feigns death, and Hudibras regards it "now, no longer safe, / To tarry the return of *Raph*" (2:3, ll. 1149–50). His departure will insure not only his own acquittal, but Ralpho's punishment for the deed and, willy-nilly, the squire's serving as the knight's proxy in the still unexecuted whipping: "For if Ralpho scape with *Whipping* now," Hudibras reasons, " 'Tis more than he can hope to do. / And that will disengage my *Conscience,* / Of th'*Obligation*" (2:3, ll. 1175–78). Thus Hudibras wins a sort of victory—momentary, to be sure, and won by deception and treachery—but this sort of victory, Butler suggests, is what we find in heroic literature.

Part 3 of *Hudibras* has not been much admired, one criticism being that (notwithstanding Butler's designation of it as the "last part") it is inconclusive. The narrative of the poem is first interrupted in canto 2 by two overly long summaries of recent history, and then it is virtually dropped to make a place for the two "heroic epistles"—one from "Hudibras to his Lady," the other, "The Ladies Answer to the Knight"—with which the poem ends. The historical accounts—one (495–998) given by a Presbyterian (identified in the "Key to Hudibras" as the Leveller, John Lilburne), the other (1011–1496) by an Independent (more certainly Anthony Ashley Cooper, Earl of Shaftesbury)—point up the "Carnal Interests" of the two dominant factions in the Puritan party; and, more generally, these accounts suggest what happens to all revolutionary movements when what "us'd to urge the Brethren on" is at last "divided, shar'd, and gone" (3:2, ll. 37–38). Bishop Burnet may have had these two passages in mind when he recommended Butler to the Princess Sophia as "the truest historian of the affairs of England from the death of Cromwell to King Charles his Restoration."[51] Then, too, the satiric approach to the heroic view of life is more direct and explicit in part 3 than in the two preceding parts of the poem. Relying less on the oblique method of rhetorical contrast and dramatic irony, Butler now requires his hero to reveal the true motives behind his "heroic" actions. When Ralpho discovers that Hudibras plans to "leave him in the *Lurch*," he goes directly to the widow, and, in hopes of marrying her himself, informs her of the knight's deceit (3:1, ll. 125–48). To punish Hudibras, who next attends the lady in person, the widow first tells him that he is sought by the ghost of Sidrophel. She then stages an "*Anti-masquerade*" of "*Furies, and Hobgoblins*" to frighten the knight into confessing not only that he ventured "*to betray, / And filch the Ladies Heart away*" (3:1, ll. 1175–76) in order to gain control of her money, but that he is a liar, a hypocrite, a breaker of vows, and a more perfect devil than the supposed spirit that is interrogating him.

This humiliation of the knight has been taken by some readers as the real conclusion of the poem. W.O.S. Sutherland, for one, says that "the finality lies in the character of Hudibras rather than in the accumulation of incident. The heroic point of view has been degraded and discredited. There remains nothing new for Hudibras to do. The poet has made his point."[52] Earl Miner, however, points out that there *is* a finality to the sequence of incidents in *Hudibras*. Though the poem is "in some sense incomplete," he finds that its incidents occur over a three-day period conforming roughly to its three parts, which in turn, he maintains, allude to the historical decades of the 1640s, 1650s, and 1660s. In part 3, then, Hudibras finds himself in the new world of the Restoration, "where he must go to law or appeal directly in hopes to gain the lady. He fails." *Hudibras,* for Miner, is about the return of Justice, not as the goddess Astraea, but as "mere woman"—as a trull and then as a widow. "Justice does rule in *Hudibras,*" he concludes, but "it rules as a signally unfunny joke."[53]

As I indicated in chapter 2, however, it is unlikely that Butler would have felt that the folly and ignorance of men are ever concluded or that his view of the reign of Charles II (especially in 1677, when part 3 was published) would include (even in the travestied form that Miner advances) the cultural values implicit in the mythic idea of "Restoration." Indeed, there is much that is new for Hudibras to try. His experience throughout the poem does not cause him to repudiate the falseness of his values but only to recognize the danger in risking life and limb to attain them. Since honor is nothing more than a word, he cannot afford to employ more than words to attain it. This method, Ralph persuades the knight, is the real heroic way—in fact as well as in fiction:

> So all their Combats now, as then,
> Are manag'd chiefly by the Pen.
> That does the Feat, with braver vigours,
> *In words at length, as well as Figures.*
> (3:3, ll. 419–22)

Henceforth, Hudibras will fight only verbal battles, and fight them where his talents in casuistry and chicanery are accepted weapons—in the courts of law and in heroic epistles. Butler's final indictment of heroic literature marks only the end of his hero's career as a knight-errant; but it constitutes a new phase in his career as a "domestick" knight.

"The Third and Last Part" of *Hudibras* also serves to draw the theme of Puritan-Independent rivalry into the total imaginative structure of the poem, reducing the apparent differences between Presbyterian and Independent, fool and knave, to a common ground. Throughout the first two parts of the poem, these differences are increasingly underscored; and they result, at the beginning of part 3, in the mutual

renunciation of Hudibras and Ralpho, a separation that is emphasized
by the contrasting historical accounts of the Puritan movement in canto
2. But at the most dramatic point in this development—the moment at
which the knight openly confesses the base motives of his "holiness"—
the action appears to reverse itself. Butler contrives this effect with
considerable care by abruptly ending the burlesque masquerade (or
"*Antimasquerade*") of the beginning of canto 1 in order to leave Hudibras "in the dark alone," unable to sleep for his aching bones, yet "still
expecting worse, and more" (3:1, l. 1329). Then, a voice "in a feeble
Tone," like the small voice of his weak conscience, speaks "these trembling words":

> . . . Unhappy Wretch,
> What hast thou gotten by this Fetch?
> Or all thy tricks in this New Trade,
> The Holy Brother-hood o'th Blade?
> By Santring still on some Adventure,
> And Growing to thy Horse a Centaure?
> . . . . . . . . . . . .
> Night is the Sabbath of Mankind
> To rest the Body and the Mind.
> Which now thou art deny'd to keep,
> And cure thy labour'd Corps with Sleep.
> (3:1, ll. 1339–52—the original in
> italics)

This voice, which continues in fits, summarizes Hudibras's "late Disas-
ters," from the engagement with the dogs and bears to his most recent
dispute with Sidrophel. So "impudently" does it "own / What I have
suffer'd for and done" (3:1, ll. 1381–82), Hudibras confesses, that it
can only belong to one of the earlier fiends who is trying now to "steal
me . . . from my self" (3:1, l. 1380).

As the reader discovers, however, this alter ego of the knight is only
Ralpho, who, in "vent'ring to betray, / Hast met with Vengeance the
same way" (3:1, ll. 1383–84), and, believing himself to be alone, he
has been lamenting his own condition. Butler does more than merely
confuse the two characters here. Knowing that Hudibras is "*too
obstinate, / To be, by me prevayl'd upon*," that "*the Devil . . . only can
prevail upon ye*" (3:3, ll. 154–55; 159–60), Ralpho is willing to damn
himself (that is, accept the role of devil) in order to damn the knight.

Hudibras, on the other hand, is willing to accept his consignment to a
place among the devils as long as it is made by an Independent whose
devilish identify is admitted; for he says to this devil,

> Tis true . . . that intercourse
> Has past between your Friends and ours,
> That as you trust us in our way,
> To raise your Members and to lay:
> We send you others of our own,
>
> .  .  .  .  .  .  .  .  .  .
>
> Have us'd all means to propagate
> Your mighty interests of State,
> Laid out our Spiritual Gifts, to further
> Your great designs of Rage and Murther.
> For if the Saints are Nam'd from Blood,
> We onl' have made that Title good,
> And if it were but in our Power,
> We should not scruple to do more.
> And not be half a Soul behind,
> Of all Dissenters of Mankind.
>
> (3:1, ll. 1529–46)

Revealed in his true nature, neither speaker is obliged to maintain a
role or to defend an opinion; and, for the first time in the poem,
Hudibras and his squire achieve a sort of harmony.

## Chapter Four

# The Argument and
# Imagery of *Hudibras*

Ordinary poetic satire, we noticed in the preceding chapter, tends to be monological. It speaks to us, that is, from a single point of view, an authorized hierarchy of values, which it implicitly affirms. If it attacks modern learning, for instance, it does so by assuming the superiority of ancient learning; antifeminist satire presupposes patriarchal authority; and so on. Butler's satire, we have seen, appears to depart from this practice. While its targets are obvious, its affirmative judgments are elusive. The most common citicism of *Hudibras* concerns its equivocal use of heroic material, which seems to be both the standard of heroism from which Puritan errantry is criticized and also the object itself of criticism. Reading *Hudibras,* we become aware of two voices, in other words, one speaking the values of traditional heroic literature, the other those of common sense, an open-ended dialogue in which the claims of the ideal and the real become mirror images of one another. Earlier, I suggested the classification *Menippean satire,* narrative that subjects traditional hierarchies to carnival inversion, as a category that includes such a medley of discourses as we find in *Hudibras.* In this chapter, I shall take up another, more inclusive descriptive class to which *Hudibras* belongs, the *satire on man,* a label that covers a putative Menippean satire like book 4 of *Gulliver's Travels* as well as formal, poetic satires like Boileau's *Satire 8* and Rochester's *Satire Against Mankind.*[1]

### Beasts and Men: Folly and Ignorance

As the name indicates, the satire on man focuses on the faults not only of particular individuals and groups—the contradictions of accepted hierarchies of value—but especially on those of the human species as a whole. As if perceiving that all received systems of judgment are privileged historical constructions, the satirist of mankind seeks the norms of nature, only to find the behavior of men less consis-

tent with these than is the behavior of animals. George Boas has
assigned the term "theriophily" to this point of view, and has traced its
source for French literature to Montaigne's *Apology for Raimond Sebond,*
to Plutarch's *Moralia,* and to the literary paradox, the brief, playful
essay that contradicts prevailing opinions on human nature.[2] References in Butler's writings to all three of these sources suggest his
awareness of the theriophilist tradition.

Near the beginning of *Hudibras,* for example, Butler refers to a
pertinent passage in Montaigne's *Apology* in which the author, "playing
with his Cat, / Complaines she thought him but an Ass" (1:1, ll. 38–
39). In canto 2 of part 2 of the poem, he specifically cites Montaigne as
a dealer in paradox, as one who makes *"true* and *false, unjust* and *just, /*
Of no use but to be discust" (ll. 9–14). Then, too, Butler's prose
observations conclude with a collection of "Contradictions" that are
only a trifle less playfully intended than the paradoxes that provided the
context of the French essayist's theriophily. We read here, for example,
that "Beasts that have no Apprehension of Death that wee can perceive,
live more according to Nature, and some Brutes are better qualifyd
with those things that wee call Virtues in our selves then men who
professe the Greatest Moritifications . . ." (152:2); that "the Breed of
Mankind is Naturally less able to help it selfe as soon as they are
producd into the world, then those of any other Creatures" (153:1); and
that "Bees and Ants seem to manage their affayrs with little less reason
of State, and more Justice than men, being wholy free from those
Distractions which the vices of Avarice Pride and Ambition produce in
Governments" (176:4). And, in his manuscript commonplace book,
Butler concludes a statement on the disorder which "Speculative
Truths" would create in world affairs with an observation that might
have come from a twentieth-century ethologist: "beasts of the same
Species that have no notion of Truth at all, live quieter among themselves then men who for the most part are not much better furnish'd;
and yet have more then they know how to make good use of" (291:3).
Though Butler's scorn of the Royal Society's experiments on animal life
is expressed in a work like the mock-scientific paper on "Dr. Charlton's
Feeling a Dog's Pulse," the observations just quoted reflect, nevertheless, the keen interest in animals that was generated by the new scientific empiricism of the age. In fact, William Horne has gone on from
this to argue that such observations express not Butler's mockery, but
his genuine interest in the New Science.[3] These observations are, unlike many others from the same source, different from those found in

Pliny's *Natural History*, that repository of fanciful animal lore that turns up again and again in works like John Lyly's *Euphues*, Robert Burton's *Anatomy of Melancholy*, and even in Pope's *Essay on Man*. It should be noted, however, that by revealing the "correspondences" between the rational and irrational links on the great chain of being, such lore finally emphasized the principle of hierarchical difference in nature. Scientific investigation, on the other hand, was beginning to undermine this sense of order by pointing out the similarities between men and beasts, and Butler may have been drawn to this data because of these ethical implications rather than for its inherent scientific interest.

Butler himself probably did not believe that animals possess reason, but then we have already observed that his view of reason made this absence no great disadvantage. Given to man not at the Creation, as tradition has it, but at the Fall, Butler believed that reason was punitive as well as redemptive, for, as we have noted, man was then "forced to drudge for that Food and Cloathing which other creatures receive freely from the Bounty of Nature" (82:4), and he was also sentenced to discover truth by his own efforts (19). But just as clothing—the peculiarly human sign of both guilt and weakness—had, in Butler's view, come to be "his greatest Indulgence" (196:3), the means of concealing human frailty, so reason—a second mark of man's fallen condition—had become the agent of his pride, the means of concealing or disguising truth when it was not to his advantage. Reason, if used as God intended it to be used—in conjunction with the senses, as the means of discovering order in nature and of ascertaining man's proper place within that order—was to be a safeguard against a recurrence of the Fall. However, as men use it, reason is both the chief weapon of knavery and the primary target at which knavery aims. For Butler, then, reason is more often a curse than a blessing, as it is more often than not used unnaturally. "'Tis not true reason I despise but yours," Rochester wrote in his *Satyr Against Mankind;* "I think Reason righted but for *Man*." Butler would have concurred with this view, and such an attitude would have led him to question the supposed inferiority of irrational animals.

We must approach Butler's theriophily somewhat indirectly by way of a passage included under the rubric "Reason" in the prose observations. "Men without Reason are much worse than Beasts," he wrote there, "because they want the End of their Creation, and fall short of that which give's them their Being; which Beasts do not, but are Relievd for that Defect, by another way of Instinct, which is nothing but a Kinde of Implicit Reason, that without understanding why, direct's them, to do, or forbeare those thinges that are agreeable, or hurtfull to their Particular Natures: while a Fool is but Half-Man, and Half-beast, is deprivd of the Advantages of both, and ha's the Benefit of Neither" (68:3). To understand fully the relationship of this remark to Butler's view of human nature, we must first recognize the broad or generic sense that the word "fool" bears in this passage. The word is used in the same way in Butler's comprehensive prose Character of "A Fool." Here we notice again the same two outstanding characteristics of the type: his relationship to an animal, and his mechanical behavior. Wanting reason, men lack the capability of self-direction—"that which give's them their Being"—and are manipulated either by others or by their own ungoverned passions. Butler's Character first describes the fool as "the skin of a man stuff'd with straw, like an alligator, that has nothing of humanity but the outside." Then, in a passage that anticipates Locke's distinction between animals and machines (the "motion" of animals "coming from within," that of machines "from without"), Butler says that the fool "is not actuated by any inward principle of his own, like an animal; but by something without him, like an engine; for he is nothing of himself, but as he is wound up, and set a going by others" (275).

Under the rubric "Wit and Folly" in the prose observations, Butler more specifically identifies folly with "Natural Madnes," a congenital deprivation of reason in man; and he contrasts it with rational nature that has in two ways been corrupted—first, with what we must call "accidental madness" ("that which men fall into by Accident or their own ungovernd Passions"), and, second, with what he himself calls "Artificiall Folly" or "Industrious Ignorance" (57:2). In this section of the observations, men without reason (natural madmen or "fools" in the specific sense) are not placed below the animals but, to their advantage, are placed on a par with them. Butler observes, for example, that the "Providence that Cloaths, and Freede's Beasts, because they know not how to help themselves, Provide's for all Sorts of Fooles, that are aequally incapable of Relieving themselves without it" (58:3). And again, under the same heading, he observes that the "Craft and Subtlety which she [Nature] ha's given to all helpless Creatures (as Hares, and Foxes)," she has also granted as a compensation for the absence of reason in natural madmen; "and hence it is that Fooles are Commonly so fortunate in the world, and wiser men so unhappy and miserable" (56:2).

On the other hand, men whose reason has been corrupted unnaturally ("accidental madmen" and the ignorant) are, throughout Butler's work, associated, to their disadvantage, with animals. The prose Characters are filled with illustrations. The "Imitator," for example, is said to have "a Kind of Monkey and Baboon Wit, that takes after some Man's Way" (136); the "Rude Man" is "the best Instance of the Truth of *Pythagoras's* Doctrine, for his Soul past through all Sorts of brute Beasts before it came to him, and still retains something of the Nature of every one" (195); the "Henpect Man" is "a Kind of preposterous Animal, that being curbed in goes with his Tail forwards" (81). Proselytes are "Cattle driven by the Priests of one Religion out of the Quarters of another" (130); a "Rabble" is "the greatest and most savage Beast in the whole World" (197); an "Inconstant" man is like a deer (243); a "Pedant," like a cock (188). The "Court-Beggar" is a dog (72); the "Bumpkin," a horse (75); the "Antiquary," a moth (27); the "Proud Man," an owl (77); the "Fantastic" a cormorant (95)—and so on.

In addition to these animal analogies of corrupted rational nature (some of which, to be sure, may be no more than instances of conventional invective), we also find a number of images of a certainly more philosophical source—those that refer to the new science of mechanics. As we have already noticed, Butler's Character of "A Fool" speaks of mechanical behavior as one of the characteristics of the man without reason; but it is also a characteristic of those who misuse reason, for in doing so, such men reject the human responsibility of self-direction (the act "which give's them their Being") and allow themselves to be governed by others or by their own passions. Descartes, I should note here, opposed the theriophilist position by arguing that animals lacked a soul and were only mechanically activated. In the *Discourse on Method,* he writes that, "if there were machines with the organs and appearance of a monky, or some other irrational animal, we should have no means of telling that they were not altogether of the same nature as those animals" (part 5). Butler, however, employs the Cartesian argument against reason in animals to criticize man's improper use of reason.[4] The Character of the "Formal Man," for example, begins with the analogy of "A Piece of Clockwork, that moves only as it is wound up and set, and not like a voluntary Agent" (237); and the same sort of figure appears in the Characters of the "Affected Man" (193) and the "Hypocrite" (218). The "Fanatic," we may recall, is described as "a Puppet Saint, that moves he knows not how, and his Ignorance is the dull leaden Weight that puts all his Parts in Motion" (128). In other

Characters, mechanical imagery is used to describe the effect of an action upon its irrational object. Thus the "Fidler" is "like the spring of a clockwork-motion, that sets all the puppets a dancing, till 'tis run down" (274); the "Musitian" "winds up souls, like watches" (293); and, since the "Knave" or Deceiver is himself a misuser of reason, he is said to be "very skilful in all the Mechanics of Cheat" (214). Hudibras even thinks of his own "wit" as "a gin" (1:3, l. 391), and for this reason, Ralpho speaks of the "mechanick Pawes" of the Puritan clergy (1:3, l. 1245); and, in part 2, the wizard Sidrophel's act of feigning death in battle is likened to the fox's trick of eluding pursuers, an action that comes "not out of Cunning, but a *Train* / Of *Atoms* justling in his Brain" (2:3, ll. 1121–22).

From these passages, then, it appears that Butler's relegation of "fools" to a place beneath that of the animals applies more to men with reason who use that faculty unnaturally or improperly than to "men without Reason" at all—that is, more to accidental madmen and to the ignorant than to natural madmen. "The theoretical—if not the psychological basis of Theriophily," says George Boas, "is that the beasts . . . are more 'natural' than man, and *hence* man's superior."[5] Animals and idiots, of course, have little ability to be anything but natural; and when, for whatever reason, they become more like human beings—as in the case of monkeys and baboons—Butler believed that they are "worse and more deformd then those Creatures that are all Beast" (7:1). Accordingly, men already handicapped by reason are placed at a still greater disadvantage by education or "Custom," as Butler calls it in the first part of the "Satyr upon the Imperfection and Abuse of Human Learning":

> For Custom, though but Usher of the Schoole
> Where Nature breede's the Body up, and Soul,
> Usurpe's a Greater Pow'r, and Interest,
> O're Man, the Heir of Reason, then Brute Beeast;
>
> . . . . . . . . . . . . . . . . . .
>
> And Traine's him up, with Rudiments more False
> Then Nature do's, her Stupid Animals
>                                              (9–16)

To human beings, reason confers both a new nature and a new freedom to achieve it. If rational men, whether consciously or unconsciously, pervert this nature, they become knaves or fools (in the comprehensive sense of the word) and "much worse than Beasts." This is not, of course, a criticism of God's creation. Butler did not categorically deny the value of reason; he vigorously attacked anti-intellectualism and philosophical skepticism by calling either one "the Modern Fals-doctrine of the Court" (17:1). Nevertheless, the misuse of reason seemed to him inevitable—and the world a place given over to knavery and folly.

The specific type of folly or perversion of human nature that is our chief concern in a reading of *Hudibras* is ignorance, the irrational behavior caused, as we have noticed, not by the want or impairment of reason (as in natural or accidental madness), but by the want of knowledge or the empirical data with which Butler believed reason properly worked. (Pope arrived at a similar notion at the beginning of Epistle 2 of *An Essay on Man,* describing man's paradoxical nature as one that is "Alike in ignorance, his reason such, / Whether he thinks too little, or too much.") Since ignorance frequently uses reason to disguise these wants, Butler conceived of it as an active rather than a passive condition, calling it, as we have seen, (*Artificial* Madness" or "*Industrious* Ignorance." In his customary imagery, reason in the ignorant man is a tailor that clothes both the mind and the world, thereby concealing human deficiencies and refashioning nature according to human desires. Just this sort of intellectual effort, Butler believed, produced the tradition of humane learning with which his hero was *internally* "accouter'd," as the poem so significantly puts it (1:1, ll. 235–36). We are informed that Hudibras *wore* his wit only on holidays "as men their best Apparel do" (1:1, l. 50), and that his linguistic habits are "a particolour'd dress"; " 'Twas *English* cut on *Greek* and *Latin,* / Like Fustian heretofore on Sattin" (1:1, ll. 97–98). Butler regarded the "Instrumentall Arts" of grammar, rhetoric, and logic as "Fopperys" (142:1) that were used to "make senseles and impertinent Reflections upon things, and having fitted them with as insignificant Tearmes, they passe for learning" (136:3). Of Aristotle, whose works for the knight are what books of chivalry were for Don Quixote, Butler observed that "his chiefest care had been to make his Systemes of her [Nature] rather Artificiall then true, and to agree among themselves very prettily, but perhaps without any great regard to Truth or Nature" (132:4). Hudibras's mind, then— as it is presented in the verse "Character" which opens the poem—is more descriptive of an intellectual type (the scholastic "realist") or an ethical type (the "ignorant" man) than of the "true blew" Presbyterian that he no less certainly represents.

In general, students of *Hudibras* have offered historical explanations

for the knight's scholasticism. John Wilders, for example, comments
that "Hudibras is typical of the early Presbyterians, many of whom
were university men. Ralpho resembles the unlettered independent
sectarians of the mid-seventeenth century who laid claim to divine
inspiration."[6] But the contrasting mental equipment of the knight and
his squire also represents two extreme forms of ignorance, or unnatural
human behavior: intellectualism and anti-intellectualism. For Butler,
as we have seen, the *natural* use of reason lies between these two
extremes. True knowlege, he believed, begins and ends with the
senses. Through perception, the understanding receives images of the
natural world; reason attempts to put these confused images into their
original order in nature; and sense, again, is called upon to verify this
mental order in the material world (64:1). Thus ignorance is likened to
a man who has replaced a lost eye with one of glass, "which though it
cannot see, can make a Shew as if it did, and is proof against al those
accidents that use to destroy true ones" (63). The use of the senses is
conspicuously absent in the thought of both Hudibras and Ralph; in
the knight, it has been replaced by the machinery of rationalism; in the
squire, by imagination.

   The knight's rationalism, his virtual blindness to the material world,
and his total commitment to the abstract intellect are the keys to our
reading of *Hudibras* as a satire on man. The importance of this character
trait might best be represented by comparing the folly of the English
knight with that of his Spanish prototype, Don Quixote. Both are
victims of illusion—the product of learning ("industrious ignorance")
in the former, and, as Butler noted, of humours (accidental madness) in
the latter (57:2). Quixote is so obsessed with the idea of chivalry that he
*sees* the images of romance in the real world: windmills actually *look* to
him like giants. But Hudibras sees little or nothing in the world; he
"forsees" (intellectually) a subversive plot against Puritanism in an
innocent bearbaiting. Logic is the mode of his folly or ignorance, and
the assumption that man is *animal rationale* is the illusion on which his
logic customarily works. Indeed, the very form of Butler's poem—and
especially the first part of it—is determined by Hudibras's mind. Part
1 begins and ends with a formal argument between the knight and his
squire about the rational nature of man. Between these two sections (or
against this background), Hudibras's battle with the bearbaiters is
told. Thus the logical demonstration of human rationality provides an
ironic context for the dramatic revelation of human nature.

# The Argument of *Hudibras,* Part 1

Hudibras's argument with Ralpho in canto 1 develops from the knight's attempt to justify prohibiting a bearbaiting. In part, his reasons are understandable, if not justifiable, for bearbaiting was prohibited by Parliament as a dangerous and ungodly pastime, and as a Puritan magistrate, Hudibras regarded it as his duty to maintain public safety (ll. 721–32) and uphold Christian piety (ll. 789–94). Another and, in the knight's mind, more important reason for stopping the bearbaiting is his quixotic interpretation of the sport as a Jesuit plot to divide the Puritan party (ll. 733–52). His reasoning to substantiate this delusion might be described as an argument that proves the natural aggressiveness of men. Hudibras argues as follows: it is not in the nature of animals, as it is in men, to fight among themselves (ll. 753–78); but men may teach animals to fight among themselves (ll. 779–88); therefore, if a dog and a bear are about to fight, men must have taught them to do so.

Hudibras's first proposition assumes that animals lack reason and the ability to "discourse," for earlier in his speech (and generally throughout the poem), he equates verbal disputation with physical fighting: "where the first does hap to be, / The last does *coincidere*" (ll. 719–20). For all its robust Englishness, *Hudibras* is above all a poem of violence, and, as William Horne points out, the principal source of this violence was the Puritan abuse of language—for Butler, "a cause of violence, a symptom of violence, and violence in itself."[7] So it is fitting that the first part of Hudibras's demonstration of the exclusively human tendency to fight should consist of the rallying cries and shibboleths that provided the "sanctifying rationale" for waging war—the "hard words" that "Set Folks together by the ears, / And made them fight, like mad or drunk": "Frail *Priviledge, Fundamental Laws . . . thorough Reformation . . . Covenant . . . Protestation,*" etc. (ll. 755–64). His second proposition assumes that, although animals lack reason, they are endowed with a sort of "wit" that enables them to "know" and to "learn," but not to conceive of a second "interest" for which men customarily fight—that is, God. This notion would have accorded with Butler's personal view of the dependence of faith upon reason; for, as he observed in his notebook, "no Irrational Creature is capable of it [faith]: and if we will not allow this, we must of necessity acknowledg that it depend upon ignorance, which is worse, for no man can believe any

thing but because he do's not know it" (67:1). Men have made gods of
Beasts, Hudibras argues; "but no Beast ever was so slight, / For man, as
for his God, to fight: / They [animals] have more wit, alas! and know /
Themselves and us better then so" (ll. 775–78). What the animals
"know" that prevents their worshipping men as gods can only be their
own nature and that of man—and that is as much as saying they know
that men are not their superiors.

Hudibras's argument in part 1 is, to say the least, self-contradictory:
it begins by assuming that men are superior to animals, and concludes
by demonstrating that they are not. But ridicule of the knight's faulty
logic is only a part of the satiric function of this argument and of the
long quarrel about Presbyterian authoritarianism that Ralpho makes of
it. More important is the fact that the argument throws a new light
upon traditional notions of the value of reason and the nature of man.
Now, it is important to recognize that Hudibras's argument is itself
purely rational; it is neither founded upon nor verified by sensory data.
It is an example, therefore, of that unnatural use of reason that Butler
called "Artificial Madness" or "Industrious Ignorance." Nevertheless,
two truths (for Butler at least) ironically emerge from Hudibras's remarks. The first is dramatically demonstrated by the action of canto 2:
reason, when used in disputation, causes strife among men; the rational
prowess with which the knight *foresees* and hopes to avert mischief
actually promotes it. The second truth, a corollary of the first, is that
men are more brutal than animals.

*Homo est animal rationale* is the traditional definition of man found in
textbooks of logic since Aristotle's time, and this axiom is customarily
opposed to an example of *animal irrationale,* traditionally the horse.
This logical commonplace provides the point of departure for Butler's
examination of man, and is therefore clearly marked in the poem. To
one as "profoundly skill'd in Analytick" (1:1, l. 66) as Hudibras, this
statement was as familiar as his own name. When Ralpho, in his
personal attack upon Presbyterianism, charges that no difference exists
between synods and bearbaitings, the knight promptly counters by
saying that "both are *Animalia . . .* but not *Rationalia*":

> For though they do agree in kind,
> Specifick difference we find,
> And can no more make *Bears* of these,
> Then prove *my horse is Socrates.*
> (1:3, ll. 1277–82)

Or again, in the courtship scene of part 2, when the knight's lady wittily
assails his virility by likening him to a *"Roan-Guelding,"* Hudibras with
perfect seriousness replies: "I am no *Horse* . . . I can argue, and discourse" (2:1, ll. 721–22). In defense of an anthropocentric world, Descartes argued that man is unique; as an understanding sign-user, he is an
inimitable creation; a beast, on the other hand—even the most sophisticated one—may be mechanically fabricated. Butler pushes this notion to
its logical limit: if reason makes men autonomous, the absence of it
makes animals mere clockwork machines. Thus, the bearbaiting episode
begins with an implicit recognition of the uniqueness of human reason;
as the knight and his squire ride out, we read that "they now begun / To
spur their living Engines on":

> For as whipp'd Tops and bandy'd Balls,
> The learned hold, are Animals:
> So Horses they affirm to be
> Mere Engines, made by Geometry,
> And were invented first from Engins.
>                           (1:2, ll. 53–59)

But the clarity of these distinctions between a rational order capable
of ethical choice and a bestial order that is not rational is only sporadic
in the poem; indeed, throughout part 1, Butler seems intent upon
blurring such distinctions. Notice, for example, the ironic effect of
Hudibras's attempt to differentiate between bears and Synod-men, between "form" determined externally and internally:

> A *Bear's* a savage Beast, of all
> Most ugly and unnatural,
> Whelpt without form, until the Dam
> Have lickt him into shape and frame:
> But all thy *light* can ne're evict
> That ever *Synod-man* was *lickt;*
> Or brought to any other fashion
> Then his own will and inclination.
>                           (1:3, ll. 1305–12)

Hudibras's beard—at various places in the poem the mark of his philosophical status, his religious commitment, or his virility—is generally
a symbol in the poem of the knight's humanity: tails, on the other
hand, symbolize bestiality. Yet we should notice how the widow man-

ages to parry Hudibras's proposal of marriage: since "*Tayls,*" she insists, "by Nature sure were meant / As well as *Beards,* for ornament," she will "never marry *man* that wants one" (2:1, ll. 743–48). To which Hudibras replies: "If she [Nature] ever gave that *boon* / To man, I'l prove that I have one; / I mean by *postulate Illation* . . . " (2:1, ll. 761–63)—that is, if necessary, he will use his reason to prove that he is an animal.

Then, in the following references to the use of language and reason (distinctively human attributes), Butler wittily confuses the orders of man and beast. Hudibras is said to speak Greek "as naturally as Pigs squeek" (1:1, l. 52); Latin was for him "no more difficile, / Then to a Blackbird 'tis to whistle" (1:1, ll. 53–54); and his linguistic fluency is described as "gabble" (1:1, l. 101). Like Mahomet, the knight was "linkt" by "fast instinct / Of wit and temper" to the ass and pigeon (1:1, ll. 230–32). Ralpho, too, "understood the speech of Birds / As well as they themselves do words" (1:1, ll. 541–42), a gift which Butler attached generally to hermetic philosophers.[8] Hudibras's highly vaunted skill in "Analytick" further confuses the species:

> He'd undertake to prove by force
> Of Argument, a Man's no Horse.
> He'd prove a Buzzard is no Fowl,
> And that a *Lord* may be an Owl;
> A Calf an *Alderman,* a Goose a *Justice,*
> And Rooks *Committee-men* and *Trustees.*
> (1:1, ll. 72–76)

In short, argument and disputation, the "*Arms* that spring from [human] *Skulls,*" place men in the class of horned beasts (1:2, ll. 439–40).

It is possible, of course, to interpret the last of these passages as merely a part of the mock-heroic machinery of the poem. However, insofar as the "heroic" is nothing more than the human, heroism assumed an ethical as well as a literary significance for Butler. Even Hudibras, in one of his more candid moments, admits "there's but the twinkling of a *Star* / Between a Man of *Peace* and *War*" (2:3, ll. 957–58). In the opening description of Hudibras, the knight is formally presented as a man living a double life: he is "amphibious" in that his knightly duties are both domestic and errant, "either for Chartel or for Warrant: / Great on the Bench, Great in the Saddle, / . . . styl'd of *War* as well as *Peace*" (1:1, ll. 21–28). But these professional alternatives are then translated into ethical and, finally, into zoological terms, and distinction becomes all but impossible:

> But here our Authors make a doubt,
> Whether he were more wise, or stout.
> Some hold the one, and some the other:
> But howsoe're they make a pother,
> The difference was so small, his Brain
> Outweigh'd his Rage but half a grain:
> .   .   .   .   .   .   .   .   .   .   .
> As *Mountaigne,* playing with his Cat,
> Complaines she thought him but an Ass,
> Much more she would sir *Hudibras.*
> (1:1, ll. 29–40)

And, if heroism or fighting makes men resemble brutes, it makes animals seem more human. Bruin, the bear, is actually ennobled by his actions in the battle. Checked on all sides by the knight and his squire, by the dogs, and by the fleeing rabble, the bear "valiantly" takes his stand, "leaving no Art untry'd, nor Trick / Of Warrior stout and Politick"; he resolves "rather than yield, / To die with honour in the field":

> But one against a multitude,
> Is more then mortal can make good.
> .   .   .   .   .   .   .   .   .   .   .
> While manfully himself he bore,
> And setting his right-foot before,
> He rais'd himself, to shew how tall
> His Person was, above them all.
> (1:3, ll. 37–84)

"Armed" (1:2, l. 259) and "clad in a Mantle *della Guer*" (1:2, l. 253), Bruin is led "to the lists" (1:2, l. 152); he is "a bold Chieftain" (1:3, l. 41), a "Champion" (1:3, l. 143), a "Warrior" (1:2, l. 152), an Achilles (1:3, ll. 139–46). The human bearbaiters, on the other hand, are mere "Auxiliary men, / That came to aid their Bretheren" (1:2, ll. 67–68).

## Animal Imagery in *Hudibras*

The frequency with which animals and men are rhetorically and poetically associated in *Hudibras* is perhaps the most telling evidence of Butler's interest in the indistinctness of human and animal nature. Animals furnish by far the largest number of images in the poem, and every human figure in part 1 is characterized by some sort of animal reference. Many of these terms are, of course, conventional forms of abuse that are commonplace in comedy. Hudibras is called an ass or an "old Cur," and he chases the bearbaiters as a cat does mice (1:3, ll. 463–64); Puritans are stubborn as mules (2:2, l. 229), and are hated worse than "dogs and snakes" (1:1, l. 742). But many are fresher than these conventional insults, or they are made to function within larger codes of bigotry. Hudibras's "amphibious" nature, for example, makes him a rat, equally at home on land or water (1:1, l. 27); at one point in the battle, Orsin "ferrets" him out for single combat (1:3, l. 236); the knight grasps his gun with a hand that resembles the talons of a goose contracting in death (1:3, ll. 525–28); and he seizes upon his lady's heart as an owl seizes upon a mouse (1:3, ll. 403–10). Talgol, the butcher-turned-bearbaiter, addresses Hudibras as "Vermine wretched, / As e're in Meazel'd Pork was hatched; / Thou Tail of Worship, that dost grow / On Rump of Justice, as of Cow" (1:2, ll. 687–90).

The sectarian Ralpho is also described as a "*Mungrel*" bred by the Puritan church (2:2, ll. 554–55), as a "Wild-foul" (1:1, ll. 507), and, because of his ability to understand only dark matters, as an owl (1:1, l. 552). The bearbaiters are regarded collectively as "tame Cattel" (1:3, 253), and are said to be infected with some "*Oestrum*" (1:2, l. 495), an insect that attacks cattle. Crowdero, the fiddler, strings his bow with a hair from his beard rather than from a horse's tail (1:2, ll. 125–28); he is called a "whelp of Sin" (1:2, l. 956); and he is addressed as "thy Curship" (1:2, l. 959). Orsin, the bearwarden, was nursed by a bear, and bred in Paris Garden (1:2, ll. 168–72). The fierce Talgol is characterized by his trade, the butchering of animals (1:2, ll. 298–326); Magnano is "fierce as forrest-Bore" (1:2, l. 335); and Trulla, the "bold Virago," is as stout as a female bear, the only species, according to philosophers, in which the female is not the weaker sex (1:2, ll. 381–82). Cerdon's disputatiousness makes him a ram or bull (1:2, l. 438); and Colon's identity has all but merged with that of his horse, except that the former "was much the rougher part, / And always had a harder heart" (1:2, ll. 451–52).

The animal analogies in *Hudibras* are not limited to those figures connected with the bearbaiting; they are attached to virtually any human type or occupation mentioned in the poem. We are told, for instance, that Orsin conducts the baiting as a lawyer antagonizes the defendant and the plaintiff in a legal action, an analogy elaborated in much the way that Ralpho later argues that Presbyterian synods are bearbaitings:

> So Lawyers, lest the *Bear* defendant,
> And Plaintiff *Dog,* should make an end on't,
> Do stave and tail with *Writs of Error,*
> *Reverse of Judgement,* and *Demurrer,*
> To let them breath awhile, and then
> Cry whoop, and set them on agen.
>
> (1:2, ll. 161–66)

In a note explaining the words "staving" and "tayling" as "terms of Art usd in the *Bear-Garden,*" Butler ironically adds that "they are us'd Metaphorically in several other Professions, for moderating, as Law, Divinity, Hectoring, etc."[9] Elsewhere, we find that an astrologer is a "Vulture" (2:3, l. 27), a Puritan a "Dog distract, or Monky sick" (1:1, ll. 209–10). Puritans make converts in the way that men catch birds, fish (2:3, ll. 7–14), or elephants—that is, with the help of a female as bait (1:2, ll. 585–88). Even men in love are like animals. Love draws them by the tails (2:1, ll. 431–32; 2:3, ll. 67–72), and rides them as horses (2:1, l. 890; 2:3, ll. 559–60). A lover is "tawed [tanned] as gentle as a Glove" (2:1, l. 880), and is, of course, given horns by an unfaithful mistress (2:2, ll. 711–12). A wife is a "clog," or manacle used on beasts (2:1, l. 654). Cupid's arrow wounds Hudibras in the "*Purtenance*" (1:3, l. 318), the "inwards" of an animal. His lady is a "Mule that flings and kicks" (1:3, ll. 331–32), and she must be taken as a bird is caught (2:1, l. 278), or as a "tumbler" (a dog) catches a coney (1:3, ll. 353–55). Human teeth and nails are "fangs" and "claws" (1:1, l. 743); skin is "hide" (1:2, l. 708), a nose a "snout" (1:3, l. 357), a beard a "mane" (2:1, l. 750). Men in general are "Moral Cattle" (2:2, l. 200).

If it be objected that I am taking these animal analogies too literally, that what is here offered as a satirical consideration of the relationship between man and beast is nothing more than conventional raillery, let us notice some examples of the reverse situation—descriptions of ani-

mals in human terms. These are less numerous than the former for the
simple reason that there are fewer animals than men in the poem;
nevertheless, such descriptions occur with sufficient frequency to suggest a satiric pattern that brutalizes men and humanizes animals. We
might, in this connection, notice the rhetorical preeminence bestowed
upon Hudibras's horse in the "Argument" to canto 1: Hudibras's *Arms
and Equipage are shown; / His Horse's Vertues, and his own*"; and later, this
horse is said to stir no more "At Spur or Switch . . . then *Spaniard*
whipt" (1:1, ll. 423–24). Butler's animals may be trained to engage in
disputes (1:1, l. 716), and are subject to the influence of the stars (1:1,
ll. 605–6); indeed, their indifference to wealth is the only distinction
(except that of religion, noted earlier) that is insisted upon in the poem
(2:1, ll. 469–70). Talgol, the butcher, is said to have "sent so vast a
Colony [of beasts] / To both the underworlds" (1:2, ll. 319–20) that he
made "many a Widow . . . and many Fatherless" (1:2, ll. 303–4). A
similar domesticating of beasts occurs in Hudibras's opening argument
against bearbaiting: is it not enough, he asks rhetorically here, that we
Puritans have risked "our Liberties, our Lives, / The Lawes, Religion,
and our Wives . . . For *Cov'nant* and the *Cause's* sake"? And yet, he
continues, in a bearbaiting, "*Dogs* and *Bears*, / As well as we, must
venture theirs (1:1, ll. 727–32). In their protection of the dog and
bear, Talgol and Orsin each strive to "deserve the Crown / Of a sav'd
Citizen," that ancient Roman recognition of service to a fellow citizen
in time of war (1:2, ll. 287–92). I might also note here that, while
Orsin had grown up among bears, Bruin " 'mong the *Cossacks* had been
bred" (1:2, l. 267).

But perhaps the most convincing evidence that Butler consciously
used language to exploit the ambiguous natures of man and beast is
found in the classical allusions and in the bits of esoteric learning that
occur in the poem. To a remarkable degree, these appear to bear upon
just such an intention. For example, Romulus, the wolf-nursed hero, is
cited as the prototype of the bearwarden, Orsin (1:2, ll. 167–68) and
Crowdero is compared to the centaur Chiron (1:2, ll. 125–32). From
the analogy of the Persian legend of a horse that proclaimed a king,
Butler invents a Staffordshire festival "where Bulls do chuse the Boldest
King / And Ruler, o're the men of string" (1:2, ll. 133–38). From the
collection of Leblanc's *Travels*, he extracts and, in a note, ironically
defends the improbability of a tall tale about a bear that "spous'd" an
Indian princess and "got on her a Race of Worthyes / As stout as any
upon earth is" (1:2, ll. 283–86). In the wooing scene of part 2,

Hudibras defends his equine virility with a reference to Semiramis of Babylon, a queen who, Butler explains in a note to the line, "is said to have receiv'd Horses into her embraces" (2:1, ll. 713–15); like Pasiphae's, her taste for animal lovers was a punishment for her indifference to men (2:1, ll. 387–98). In part 1, learned antiquaries are cited to testify that man is the youngest of the creatures—"For Beasts, when man was but a piece / Of earth himself, did th' earth possess" (1:2, ll. 467–73); and Hudibras's lady summons "*Philosophers* of late" to establish that "Men have fower legs by *Nature*," amplifying her remarks with an account of a German boy who was adopted by wolves, "and growing down t'a man, was wont / With *Wolves* upon all four to hunt" (2:1, ll. 725–32).

The combined effect of many of these images and allusions, as I have been suggesting, is to provide a sort of naturalistic accompaniment to the battle between Hudibras and the bearbaiters. These references encourage the reader, by the middle of canto 3 in part 1, to believe that men behave like animals and that reason—such as that used earlier by Hudibras to prove the distinctiveness of man—leads to quarrelsomeness and brutishness. That the knight and his squire should at this point renew their earlier argument is a further joke at the expense of human nature, for neither imagination nor reason has yet led them to the truth that the bear has learned through simple experience:

> that they [men]
> For whom h'had fought so many a fray,
> And serv'd with loss of bloud so long,
> Should offer such inhumane wrong.
> (1:1, ll. 893–96)

It may appear that Ralpho, whose fanciful use of animal analogies for men exceeds any thus far demonstrated, has also learned this truth: at one point, he remarks that although "*Bears* naturally are beasts of Prey, / That live by rapine, so do they [synods]" (1:3, ll. 1123–24); and that "the difference is, The one fights with / The Tongue, the other with the Teeth" (1:3, ll. 1107–08); moreover, he is contemptuous of the knight's rationalist approach to the world, calling it "A fort of Errour, to ensconce / Absurdity and ignorance" (1:3, ll. 1349–50). But Ralpho's position is also a case of special pleading, directed not at men in general, but only at Presbyterians: "*Saints* themselves are brought to stake," he says, and "expos'd to *Scribes* and *Presbyters*, / Instead of

*Mastive-dogs* and *Curs;* / Then whom th' have less humanity, / For these at souls of men will flie" (1:3, ll. 1111–16). Though it may appear to voice Butler's own views, Ralpho's argument rests upon neither experience nor reason, but upon a supernatural "gift" of inspiration. He regards the knight's rational prowess as

> An Art t'incumber *Gifts* and wit,
> And render both for nothing fit;
> Makes *light* unactive, dull and troubled,
> Like little David in Saul's doublet.
>                              (1:3, ll. 1343–46).

Ralpho's indictment of rational man is, therefore, just as partial as Hudibras's defense of him; and the squire's view serves as a means of concealing the speaker's own inhumanity while it attributes bestiality to those whose opinions differ from his own. Ralpho earns his place beside the knight in the stocks at the end of part 1.

This confinement of Hudibras and Ralpho is Butler's final act of comic revenge against mankind. Incapable now of public mischief (the stocks were described earlier in the poem as a harness that renders the body sensitive to "Spur and Switch, / As if 'twere ridden Post by Witch" [1:2, ll. 1157–58]), rational man ironically condemns himself. Interpreting literally Ralpho's identification of Presbyters with "*Bears* and *Dogs* and *Bearwards* too," Hudibras fails to see the truth of what he logically denies: that rational man is "a strange *Chimaera* of Beasts and Men, / Made up of pieces Heterogene, / Such as in Nature never met . . ." (1:3, ll. 1315–19). For the careful reader of part 1 of *Hudibras*, however, no amount of ratiocination can make him appear otherwise.

## Male Chauvinism in *Hudibras*, Parts 2 and 3

In part 1 of *Hudibras*, then, Butler satirized mankind by elaborating upon the ambiguous relations between rational man and the irrational beast. But what of the remainder of the poem, the conclusion of which took fifteen years to appear? Did the satirist relent in his attack upon general human nature as the memories of Commonwealth cruelty and hypocrisy receded? In parts 2 and 3, Butler dropped the story of Hudibras's battle with the bearbaiters, and, as I have related, introduced the affair of the knight's wooing of a widow—moved, as he says, from the clash of "rusty Steel" in war to the "more gentle stile" of love. But, although a stronger relationship exists between parts 2 and 3 than between either of these sequels and part 1 (or, to put it more precisely, although the narrative coherence of part 3 is more dependent upon part 2 than that of part 2 is upon its predecessor), the general direction of the original satire remains unchanged in the latter parts. Human rationality or reason abstracted from the checks and balance of the senses is still the target. But the satirical stance appears to be feminist rather than theriophilist; reason is judged now in relation to feminine common sense rather than to animal instinct. Butler assumes that his reader is at least aware of what we would call the male chauvinism of the seventeenth century—he expects us to identify human reason as masculine reason. Thus, as the satire of part 1 aims to elevate animals over men, that of parts 2 and 3 aims to elevate women over men.

Traditionally, of course, woman occupied a place on the great chain of being somewhat below man. True, a new note was beginning to be heard in some seventeenth-century considerations of marriage. In *Paradise Lost,* Milton allowed Adam to complain to God about the incompleteness of a world without woman in words that at least suggest the idea of equality:

> Among unequals what society
> Can sort, what harmony or true delight?
> Which must be mutual, in proportion due
> Giv'n and receiv'd
>
> > (8: 383–86)

and Hudibras's lady also argues from the assumption that equality is a necessary condition for marriage:

> . . . What does a *Match* imply
> But *likeness* and *equality?*
> I know you cannot think mee fit,
> To be the *Yoke-fellow* of your *Wit:*
> Nor take one of so mean *Deserts,*
> To be the *Partner* of your *Parts.*
> > (2:1, ll. 669–74)

But these speeches are special cases: the context of Adam's words concerns the impropriety of human "conversation" between man and beast; Adam longs for companionship "fit to participate / All rational delight, wherein the brute / Cannot be human consort" (*PL* 8: 389–92). And

Butler's lady is parrying the knight's proposal of marriage. Milton himself, who justified divorce on the grounds of an "unconversing inability of *minde*" in either partner in marriage, nevertheless reflected the male supremacist bias of his era by speaking of man as "the perfeter sex." Cultural historians tell us that the political activities of women during the Civil War years gave them a taste of sexual freedom that helped to undermine the traditional hierarchy of the family, but, according to Lawrence Stone, this effect was short-lived: along with the Restoration of monarchy came a restoration of the old pattern of domestic authority.[10] Milton makes it abundantly clear in *Paradise Lost* that order in the domestic state depends upon the authority residing in the hands of the physically and intellectually superior husband. To deny the subordinate status of women, a spokesman for the prevailing view wrote in 1635, "is to resist the Councell of the Highest."[11] Yet this is precisely what Butler appears to be doing in *Hudibras*. Whereas other seventeenth- and eighteenth-century writers invoke the myth of the Amazon ("the ruling woman or the masculineized woman who exemplifies man's fear of uselessness") in order to disarm or neutralize it, Butler, in Felicity Nussbaum's words, "plays with those expectations and turns them upside-down."[12] Butler gives Trulla, the fierce virago-bearbaiter, greater physical strength and courage than either Hudibras or her male counterparts, and he makes the craft and common sense of the hero's lady triumph over the masculine learning and intellect of her lover.

Butler's protofeminism is problematic, however. Earl Miner, who first drew serious attention to the role of women in the poem, is quite properly ambivalent on the question: he argues that Butler's "advocacy of female superiority"—"so extraordinary and so persistent that it must be considered a central theme"—causes us nevertheless, to suspect him of "a yet worse misogyny" in permitting "the sickliest of ideals to take strength in transvestism."[13] William Horne's more narrowly focused investigation of "the women question" in the poem is no less inconclusive. Unable to choose between a "Butler-who-is-almost-feminist" and one who is "an unreconstructed sexist," Horne reads the "marriage debate" between the knight and the widow as an expression of Butler's inability to endorse either the traditional patriarchal model for marriage or the Restoration "contractual model, the idea that marriage was at base no more than an economic and legal arrangement."[14] But the role of men and women in the poem is also related to Butler's attitude toward heroic literature and romance.

As we have already noticed, Butler regarded the effect of these fictions as anything but salutary, believing that images of masculine virtue encouraged not emulation—as apologists for the heroic optimistically argued—but moral lassitude and complacency in its readers. On the other hand, he regarded the humiliating images of men found in satires and lampoons as morally efficacious. The latter are "more True" than the former, and are therefore "capable of doing . . . more good," he wrote in the prose observations, "for Panegyriques being nothing but Polite Flattery never did any" (163:2). Thus, in masking the real physical and spiritual weaknesses of men, the assumptions and conventions of heroic fiction also supported the traditional belief in masculine superiority. And this belief was reinforced by another romantic cliché, that of the saintly but vulnerable female. The appearance, in canto 2 of part 2, of a skimmington—a social ritual performed "when o're the Breeches greedy *Women* / Fight, to extend their vast *Dominion*" (ll. 699–700),[15] and thus designed both to exorcise the tendencies of women to rebel against their subordinate position and to shame the men who allowed them to do so—testifies to the persistence of these myths in the world of the poem. In obstructing the progress of the skimmington, then, Hudibras errs in two ways: he mistakes its female victim—a shrew who belongs in popular antifeminist literature—for the idealized lady of courtly romance, or for her Commonwealth counterpart—one who "fixt" her man "constant to the *Party*, / With motives powerful, and *hearty*" (ll. 785–86); but he also attacks an essentially conservative folk ritual aimed at preserving the hierarchy on which his own fancied authority depends. The promoters of the skimmington, enforcers of masculine supremacy, are on Hudibras's side.

Hudibras makes a similar mistake in his dealings with the widow. He assumes that this lady will respect the rules of romance, that she will exhibit the conventional submissiveness of her type in order to give him the opportunity to display his assumed superiority. But such an opportunity—the conventional testing of a knight—is pointless, and the lady knows it; she is, after all, an experienced widow. Quite literally, she plays the role of the "lady" of romance—serving as the embodiment of Hudibras's desire and as the determiner of his words and actions—and she does so only to expose his weaknesses. Indeed, she is the satiric intelligence of the second and third parts of the poem. In part 1, Butler, the "satirist" or narrator, is himself the stage director, equipping his hero with "sufficient" reason and then retiring to the wings to watch him bring about his own undoing. But in the two following parts of the poem, Hudibras's mistress, the unnamed widow, is even more directly involved in the exposure of the knight. Endowed with wealth and with knowledge of the character of men, she becomes a baited trap for the knight when she obtains, at the opening of part 2, his release from the stocks at a price (true honor) that she knows he cannot pay, and thereby prompts him to a course of deception that she can expose whenever she pleases.

Quite understandably, Hudibras is the defender of the traditional fictions about the sexes. Forced to surrender to the ignominy of the stocks by one woman and then to purchase freedom at the equally repugnant terms of another, the knight draws a final sanction of unjustified self-esteem from the orthodox scale of being. Thus, the argument of Hudibras's "Heroical Epistle" to the widow rests on the premise that "Women first were made for Men, / Not Men for them" (ll. 273–74). Milton, too, in the *Doctrine and Discipline of Divorce,* maintained that "woman was created for man, and not man for woman"[16]; and, in *Tetrachordon,* he deduced from this premise a peculiarly masculine ground for divorce: "Seeing woman was purposely made for man . . . it cannot stand before the breath of this divine utterance, that man . . . joyning to himself for his intended good and solace an inferiour sexe, should so becom her thrall, whose wilfulness or inability to be a wife frustrates the occasionall end of her creation, but that he may acquitt himself to freedom by his naturall birthright, and that indeleble character of priority which God crown'd him with."[17] And if masculine "priority" permits a man to sever the bonds of matrimony, it can also, Hudibras reasons, guarantee his right to tie them—even if the inferior woman in question is opposed to the idea. Reason, in other words, can have it both ways. "It follows then," the knight goes on in his letter to the lady,

> That Men have right to every one,
> And they no freedom of their own:
> [That] . . . Men have pow'r to chuse,
> But they no Charter to refuse:
>
> .   .   .   .   .   .   .   .   .
>
> And that you ought to take that course,
> As we take you *for Bett'r or worse*
> And Gratefully submit to those,
> Who you, before another chose.
> ("Hudibras to His Lady," ll. 273–86)

These lines seem strangely direct language (reaching at times even libertine positions) for the hypocritical rhetorician who never opened his mouth but "out there flew a Trope." But the libertine does not try to justify his nature, and Hudibras tries to do little else in his letter. It is significant that the knight's apology for masculine supremacy is part of a longer apology for his own use of deception in courtship. Casuistry and ratiocination, like the exercise of the masculine will, are the "prerogatives" of rational men. Hudibras therefore locates the cause of his present disgrace (the widow has both rejected his proposal of marriage and exposed him as a liar) not in himself, but in the collapse of the established sexual hierarchy:

> . . . why should every Savage Beast
> Exceed his *Great Lord's Interest?*
> Have freer Pow'r, then he, in *Grace,*
> *And Nature,* o're the Creature has?
> Because the Laws, he since has made,
> Have cut off all the Pow'r he had,
> Retrench'd the absolute Dominion
> That Nature gave him, over Woman.
> ("Hudibras to His Lady,"
> ll. 287–94)

The prerogatives of "*Grace and Nature*" make men the lords of women as well as of animals. Masculine reason not only justifies its own faults; it makes feminine resistance to its arguments a violation of natural law.

But while Hudibras and his brethren strive to maintain the prerogatives guaranteed them by tradition, the women in the poem make it quite clear that the traditional sexual hierarchy is no reflection of the relative capabilities of men and women. The bearbaiting Trulla wins Hudibras's sword and forces him to wear her petticoat; and Hudibras's lady, who senses the ironic possibilities in being able to rescue her knight from the stocks, attends him as a "gossip" assists at the "labour" of an expectant mother, although she hesitates to *deliver* him because romance offers no precedent for such a demonstration of feminine ability.

Thus, as the imagery of part 1 tended to brutalize men and humanize animals, that of parts 2 and 3 tends to feminize men and masculinize women. Intellectually, as well as physically, the women outclass the men in the poem—and they manage to do so even with the imperfect rational powers that their age assigned them. In "The Ladies Answer to the Knight," the satirical climax of the poem, the widow exposes the dishonesty not only of Hudibras's marital demands, but also of the concept of masculine "priority" that lies behind them. Hudibras's revealed dishonesty is not a new discovery on her part; but it becomes the basis of her demonstration that feminine intuition and experience are better at detecting fraud than masculine reason is at perpetrating it. Wealth is the real incentive of her "lover's" courtship, she says in a witty critique of amatory convention: " 'Tis not those Orient Pearl's our Teeth . . . But those we wear about our Necks, / Produce those Amorous Effects" ("The Ladies Answer," ll. 65–68); and, she continues, "these Love-tricks I've been vers't in so, / That all their sly *Intrigues,* I know" (ll. 73–74). But the widow is not offended by the economic motives of marriage; she herself is a practical materialist:

> [Love,] where there's Substance, for it's Ground,
> Cannot but be more Firm, and Sound,
> Then that which has the slighter Basis,
> Of *Airey virtue, wit, and graces.*
>                    ("The Ladies Answer," ll. 105–08)

As Ruth Nevo shrewdly observes, "the whole marriage debate between Hudibras and the Widow, though interwoven with motifs familiar in such debates since the Middle Ages, is firmly grounded, in both parties to the debate, upon the assertion of the economic nature of the institution."[18] Hudibras's interest in her money "is Right," she concedes; it is "the Course, / You take to do't, by Fraud, or Force" (ll. 149–50) that arouses her contempt.

What prompts the widow to answer the knight at all is less her desire for personal victory over a man she has never taken seriously than the opportunity to strike at reason's self-begotten fiction of masculine power—a fiction that this representative man personifies in his every act and word. She would show all men that women cannot be tricked or coerced; that the power sanctioned by their rationally contrived myth of superiority is illusory—Hudibras, the man, testifies to its falsity; and that real power consists in the acceptance of often unflattering truths about human nature. Thus, the widow is quite willing to accept the role that men have given her sex—that of the passionate seductress of reason; in fact, she can even accept the biblical premise of this view, for she recognizes that the real power in a world of mortals is sexuality, not rationality:

> Though Women first were made for Men,
> Yet Men were made for them agen:
> For when (*out-witted by his Wife*)
> Man first turn'd Tenant, but, *for life,*
> If Women had not Interven'd,
> How soon had Mankind had an end?
>
> . . . . . . . . . . .
>
> Then where's your Liberty of Choyce,
> And our unnatural No-voyce?
>           ("The Ladies Answer, ll. 239–48)

It is not the rational disputation of men, she says, but "our more *Pow'rful Eloquence*," that manages "things of Greatest weight, / In all the world's *Affairs of State*" (ll. 294–96).

Philip Harth has characterized the view we have taken here as "male chauvinism with a vengeance!": "seventeenth-century Englishmen may well have been sexist in many of their attitudes, but they certainly never carried them to such a pitch as that."[19] Harth's comment may tell us more about the susceptibilities of twentieth-century critics than about seventeenth-century attitudes toward women. It is difficult, in fact, to generalize about Butler's personal views on women. His occasional observations outside *Hudibras* provide contradictory opinions. Most often, perhaps, these reflect the antifeminist prejudices of his age. Butler does not, for instance, reflect the idea that women have no souls; but, in the following lines, he credits the idea to others:

> The Soules of women are so small
> That Some believe th' have none at all;
> Or, if they have, Like Cripples, still
> Th' ave but one facu[l]ty, the Will;
> The other two are quite layd by
> To make up one great Tyranny:
> And though their Passions have most Powr,
> They are (like Turkes) but slaves the more
> To th' Abs'lute will, that with a breath
> Has Sovrain Powr of life and Death.
> And, as it's little Interests move,
> Can turne 'em all to Hate or love,
> For nothing in a Moment turn
> To Frantique Love, Disdain, and Scorn,
> And make that Love degenerate
> T' as great extremity of Hate

> And Hate againe, and Scorn, and Piques
> To Flames, and Raptures, and Love-Tricks.[20]

At the same time, however, we must also notice that such remarks by Butler often appear in contradiction to one another—an indication possibly of a weakening of prejudice, or of the strain involved in asserting it. Butler belittles women as the "weaker vessels," but he also appears to fear them for their sexual power or "Naturall Arts" (96:3), an inconsistency that reflects both the tradition that Satan chose Eve for his agent in Eden, and the current suspicion that priests use women as their chief means of proselytizing in families (52). Though Butler attempts to naturalize the salaciousness of women (as the motive of procreation [91:7]), he also observes that they differ in this respect from the lower creatures in whom it is the male, not the female, that is "always ready to generate" (183:4). Butler would have women judged by a more general understanding than the conventional morality that equated virtue with chastity and honor with "only not being whores"; he implies that they are capable of more than "a mere Negative Continence" that may itself become the source of feminine pride and an excuse for many other faults attributed to the sex (74:5).

But although Butler may often echo his age's estimate of feminine reason, he did not share its faith in the assumed intellectual and moral superiority conferred by masculine reason. I have already spoken of his attitude toward reason—that, though it is the means of surviving in a world of evil, it is also the root of human folly and villainy. The very faculty that can prevent the recurrence of Adam's original delusion had become through pride the means of man's subsequent self-delusion or ignorance. For this reason, Butler may at least satirically entertain the notion that the instinctive beast (56:2) or the lucky natural fool (who is guided by some sort of special providence [58:3]) is more than an equal match for rational man. And in *Hudibras,* I am suggesting, he makes a similar concession about the unreasonable, but cunning and wily, woman who is endowed with "Naturall Arts" of her own for turning men's heads (96:3). As for marriage, is that state of harmony guaranteed by the authority of a rational husband? Butler regarded marriage not as a state of order but as a condition of perpetual strife—as a conflict between the pride of masculine reason and the even stronger power of the feminine senses and will:

> Hence 'tis, they are no sooner made one Flesh,
> And both compounded int' a civil mesh;

> But Sexes next become the sole debate,
> And which has greater right to this, or that;
> Or whether 'tis Obedience, or Dominion
> That Man can claim a title to, or Woman,
> Untill the Issue has been fairly try'd,
> And legally found oftest for the bride,
> Who can reduce the most imperious Brave
> To be her Drudge, and Utensil, and Slave:
> To Husband takes the Idiot during life
> And makes him but a Helper to his wife.[21]

The moral and physical victories of the women in *Hudibras,* then, are part of the strategy of Butler's satire against man—*animal rationale.* In his *Satyr Against Mankind,* Rochester said he would "be a *Dog,* a *Monkey,* or a *Bear,* / Or any thing but that vain *Animal,* / Who is so proud of being rational." In part 1 of *Hudibras,* Butler used Rochester's dog and bear to ridicule man's pride in reason; in parts 2 and 3, he takes up his "any thing" and makes it a woman to achieve this end.

## Carnival Form in *Hudibras*

So far, I have dealt with *Hudibras* as a satire of the intellectual and spiritual pretensions of human beings in general and of Puritans in particular. I have also noted Butler's use of parodic inversion as a satirical technique for turning upside-down the received hierarchies of man and beast, men and women, and for turning inside-out the physical side of the man of mind and spirit in the exposure of Puritan hypocrisy. If Butler appears to respect Trulla and the widow but condemns Hudibras, the reason is that the women in the poem accept what they are and the man does not; and what the characters accept or deny is the *carnal* side of their nature, one of the "hard words" in the Puritan vocabulary and one that recurs frequently as a modifier in the language of *Hudibras* (as in "carnal hour-glass," "carnal man," "carnal crabats," "carnal swine," "carnal Jerkin," "carnal interests," "carnal orders," "carnal reason"). In dealing with the argument of the poem, I have necessarily emphasized the critical function of the satire, its exhibition of what Hudibras *is not:* he is not honest, not brave, not wise—in a word, not a "saint." But the satire also exhibits what Hudibras *is.* At the lowest social and linguistic level of the poem, the level of street-cries and "rough music" and marketplace Billingsgate, in jokes about bums and rumps and fundament, and in images of food and bruised flesh and bone-breaking misrule, the knight is revealed not only as carnal man, but as carnival man. *Hudibras,* we shall yet see, parodies the forms of popular carnival, the traditional means of celebrating the flesh, as a way of exposing and thus satirizing the Puritan body.

Butler makes the connection between carnival and Puritan hypocrisy explicit in one of his prose observations:

Incontinence is a less Scandalous Sin in Clergy-men then Drinking, because it is manag'd with greater Privacy, then the other Iniquity, which is apt to expose them to greater Freedom, and tempt them naturally, to venture too far, without their Necessary Guard of Hypocrisy, without which they are in perpet- uall Danger of being Discoverd, that is to say, undon. The Flesh has a greater advantage against the Spirit, in zealots then any other Sort of men, For their natural inclinations that can Indure nothing that is settled, and injoyned, must of Necessity posses them, with as great and earnest longings to breake Commandments and violate the Laws of God with the same zeal and eagernes as they do the Laws of the Land. For that extraordinary and supercilious Reservdnes which he always puts on in Publique, is not to conceal nothing, but hide something else that is worse, from the sight of the world. For he that is Innocent is not so apt to stand always upon his guard, as one that is guilty and perpetually in fear of being discoverd. And therefore this outward stiff Mortification dos really appear to be but a kinde of Spiritual Carnevall, in which all men are allowed to use all manner of Freedom under a Vizard.
(213)

The specific carnival analogy drawn here is, of course, the masquerade, an attenuated chamber version of marketplace carnival which Mikhail Bakhtin associates with the emergence of bourgeois individualism in the seventeenth century; even so, the mask, or "Vizard," may be re- garded as a mark of alienation from oneself.[22] As Terry Castle points out, an obligatory convention of the masquerade is that one appear as one's opposite: masquerade "defined a second self at the farthest remove from the actual. It was, in short, ironic."[23] In the case of Hudibras, the man of flesh behind the mask of spirit, it is travesty.

More interesting than this rather obvious analogy between hypocrisy and masquerade, however, is Butler's invention of the contradictory phrase "Spiritual Carnevall" and the discussion of carnival psychology that suggested it. The main point of the observation is that hypocrisy and traditional folk carnival are both motivated by physical appetites and the desire for freedom, the only difference being the greater strength of these energies in the zealot-hypocrite. Butler probably remembered that pre-Commonwealth England licensed carnival and other forms of popular misrule as a sort of safety valve for dangerous social energies, misrule actually helping to preserve the hierarchies they appeared to be overthrowing. Butler, though, would probably not have endorsed this theory of carnival; indeed, the passage under consideration points out a fallacy in it. Traditional carnival becomes "Spiritual Carnevall" when it encounters physical energies of disproportionate strength; when the spectacle of carnival indulgence fails to contain the energies of the zealot, carnival spectacle becomes a means of concealment and denial. It becomes hypocrisy. The innocence of traditional carnival misrule was guaranteed by its total visibility, its sharply defined limits, and yet its ultimate open-endedness. Popular carnival, as Bakhtin explains it, celebrated change, the unfinished potential of life; its participating bodies outgrow themselves, transgress their own limits, thereby breaking down hierarchic distinctions (*Rabelais and His World*, 39–40). But these liberties were sanctioned only on specific days of the year and within the established boundaries of the marketplace square. "Spiritual Carnevall" necessarily perverts these ends. Its danger lies in its mask of secrecy, which covertly licenses greater freedom by appearing to deny the body than traditional carnival does by openly indulging it; and in doing so, "Spiritual Carnevall" guarantees its own permanence, abolishing the boundary between the festive world of play and the real world so that revolution becomes a fact and at the same time fixes the distinctions created in its own hegemony.

Butler's observation on hypocrisy argues that the man of spirit, the Puritan "Saint," is actually an hypertrophied man of flesh, a distortion of carnival man. *Hudibras* is a satirical demonstration of this idea. The comic action of the poem redefines a representative of the Puritan "Spiritual Carnevall" as the central figure of popular carnival—exposes the knight first as the fool-become-carnival-king, then as the uncrowned, reluctant carnival-clown, and finally as an ordinary man with extraordinary appetites. Moreover, since carnival remains open to the processes of history, the carnival action of the poem may be understood as Butler's own comment on the events of his time. Ricardo Quintana has suggested that Butler thought of the Commonwealth as a romance and the Restoration as a heroic poem; quite possibly, he also regarded both events as revolutions in the perennial cycle of carnival. Indeed, much of the poem that has been understood solely in terms of a learned tradition of heroic parody may also be read in terms of the popular tradition of carnival festivity and misrule. Butler's opening description of the bearbaiting as an old form of "Recreating" or renewal resurrected by the common people places this sport among those expressions of carnival spirit that Bakhtin calls the "carnivalesque":

> To this Town People did repair
> On dayes of Market or of Fair,
> And to crack'd Fiddle and hoarse Tabor
> In merriment did drudge and labour:
> But now a sport more formidable
> Had rak'd together Village rabble.
> 'Twas an old way of Recreating,
> Which learned Butchers call *Bear-baiting*.
> (1:1, ll. 666–72)

Crowdero, the fiddling leader of the bearbaiters, is associated with festivity by his wooden leg, the legacy, we are told, of an unsuccessful attempt to be crowned king of the minstrels of Staffordshire (1:2, ll. 133–42). Hudibras, who condemns the sport as a "vain, untriumphable fray" (1:2, l. 502), speaks as both a Puritan who can find no victory possible in an internecine feud among the saints, and as a hero of romance for whom battle unglamorized by the "Law of Arms" is mere butchery. As a carnival ritual, the bearbaiting expresses an ideology that is inimical to both of these "official" views. To Hudibras, who speaks for individual effort and serious action—action engaged in once-and-for-all, completed in fixed certainty—the bearbaiting is indeed "untriumphable," a repeated, communal action, incomplete, open-ended, suspending all seriousness.

But if Hudibras and the bearbaiters are so thoroughly differentiated as to stand in opposition to one another as representatives of official order and unofficial misrule, other features of the poem connect the hero to the popular carnival tradition. The most prominent of these is the physical appearance of the knight. Take away Sir Hudibras's scholastic and chivalric pretensions, strip him of the trappings of altar and bench, and what remains is the carnival fat-man, a belly "cramm'd with . . . White-pot, Butter-milk, and Curds" and breeches "lin'd with many a piece / Of Ammunition-Bred and Cheese, / And fat Black-puddings" (1:1, ll. 297, 311–13). Notwithstanding his recognized relation to Don Quixote, the English knight owes his most prominent physical characteristic to Sancho Panza, who, Bakhtin points out, transmitted the carnival spirit into Cervantes's novel: Sancho's potbelly is the "bodily grave . . . dug for Don Quixote's abstract and deadened idealism . . . the popular corrective of laughter applied to the narrow-minded seriousness of the [knight's] spiritual pretense" (*Rabelais and His World,* 22). Butler, who made no effort to conceal his borrowings from *Don Quixote,* gave this carnival obesity not to Ralpho, the Hudibrastic counterpart of the Cervantean squire, but to Sir Hudibras himself, thereby combining Cervantes's man of spirit and man of flesh in the literal representation of "Spiritual Carnevall."

Deprived, then, of any carnival difference from Hudibras, the Independent Ralpho functions chiefly in terms of his doctrinal difference from the Presbyterian knight. This modification of the Cervantean model (which allowed Sancho and Quixote to play out their carnival difference in a sort of festive Battle of Carnival and Lent) allows Butler's squire to function as a particularly candid commentator on the similarities between the "Spiritual Carnevall" in which the knight participates and the popular carnival he opposes, but secretly enjoys. After Hudibras's initial victory over Crowdero, for instance, Ralpho reminds the knight that the luxuries of the flesh enjoyed by the bearbaiters—"Their Dogs, their Horses, Whores and Dice, / Their Riots, Revels, Masks, Delights, / Pimps, Buffons, Fidlers, Parasites"—are rightfully *"th' Creature* [comforts]" of the Saint (1:2, ll. 1010–17). The motivation of the Presbyterian knight, in other words, is no less carnal than that of the bearbaiters. Ralpho knows his master for the hypocrite he is—"*Clerick* before, and *Lay* behind" (1:3, ll. 1224–26).

Because bearbaiting violated an actual Parliamentary ordinance prohibiting popular sports, Hudibras justifies his interference in it primarily on political grounds. He objects to this "old way of Recreating" as a threat to established order (an order that validates his own authority in it), speaks of it as a *"Machiavilian* Plot . . . to divide / The well-affected" (1:1, ll. 733–38), and interprets its very form—as the bear "wheels about, / And overturns the Rabblerout" (1:1, ll. 681–82)—as the sign of revolution. From Ralpho's fundamentalist point of view, however, anything not explicitly recorded in scripture is simply "carnal, and of man's creating" and "therefore unlawful and a sin" (1:1, ll. 800–803). Ralpho, then, sees no difference between the bearbaiting (a *"Babylonish* sport," in his view) and the Presbyterian hierarchical structure it threatens:

> . . . both are so near of kin,
> And like in all, as well as sin,
> That put them in a bag and shake 'em,
> Your self o'th' sudden would mistake 'em,
> And not know which is which, unless
> You measure by their Wickedness:
> For 'tis not hard t'imagine whether
> O'th' two is worst, though I name neither.
>                                   (1:1, ll. 831–39)

Ralpho's exposure of the carnival origins of the knight and his religion establishes the main carnival action of part 1 of the poem. By the time the squire returns to this line of argument in canto 3, Hudibras will have performed the ritual of the traditional carnival clown; he will have both led the vanquished Crowdero "in triumph . . . through the Town" (1:2, ll. 1113–66) and himself been led backwards on his horse, beaten and physically abused, and forced to wear the mantle of his female conqueror, Trulla (1:3, ll. 919–21, 961–82). In Bakhtin's analysis of this pattern of traditional carnival imagery, physical abuse is not personal chastisement, but symbolic action; it is "equivalent to a change of costume, to a metamorphosis": "The clown was first disguised as a king, but once his reign had come to an end his costume was changed, 'travestied,' to turn him once more into a clown. . . . Abuse reveals the other, true face of the absurd, it tears off his disguise and mask. It is the king's uncrowning" (*Rabelais and His World*, 197). Ralpho's remarks in canto 3 on the carnival nature of Hudibras's actions and of Presbyterian government reflect this cycle of crowning and uncrowning, the carnival inversion of already inverted worlds. Like the carnival dummy of the dying year, Hudibras represents temporal change, though in his case a specifically historical change; his fortunes fluctuate, Ralpho observes, with the turning over of 'a *Carnal Hourglass*" (1:3, ll. 1062). The victor of "a *Bear* and *Rabble*" becomes the wearer of "a *Cap* and *Bauble*" (1:3, ll. 1067–68): the carnival king becomes the carnival clown. Arguing that "*Synods* are mystical Bear gardens"[24]—i.e., spiritual carnivals (1:3, l. 1095)—Ralpho places the figures of all Presbyterian authority, the "bishops" of every English hamlet who command "the *Keies* for Cheese and Bacon" (1:3, ll. 1208–9), in a succession of uncrowned carnival fatmen stretching from the butcher clerks of the heathen priesthood (1:3, ll. 1189–91) to the "Tithe-pig-Metropolitan" of Rome (1:3, ll. 1205–6). For Ralpho, carnival is the archetype of this historical process; for Butler, historical change itself is merely carnival illusion.

The carnival of Butler's poem does not end with the uncrowning of Hudibras and the coronation of Trulla. Official hierarchies remain in suspension as more women gain ascendency over men; popular misrule continues to reign in the skimmington; and Hudibras, his carnality exposed by Ralpho and the bearbaiters, must try to evade both the summary popular justice of "*Py-powder*" administered at fairs and markets (2:2, l. 306) and the festive whipping which, as wooer of the widow, he foolishly promises to undergo. Butler's burlesque of the conventions of romance in part 2 of the poem is, like his parody of heroic conventions in part 1, a continual play with the forms of popular carnival.

The widow stands at the center of this carnivalized romance, a curiously disembodied figure whose fatal attraction upon her "spiritual" lover completes his self-disclosure as a creature of little more than body. The widow's relation to the carnival action she instigates is ambiguous. Her rescue of the knight from the stocks, her ability to manipulate him in argument, and, later, her argument for inversion of the sexual hierarchy align her with Trulla and the "unruly ruling woman"[25] of the skimmington, a popular spectacle of the festive tradition. Ralpho, too, places her in the company of the carnal when he tells the knight "She's of the *Wicked,* as I guess, / B'her *looks,* her *language,* and her *dress*" (2:2, ll. 251–52), although in her first appearance (when she views Hudibras in the stocks), she makes her allegiance known not by these superficial signs, but by her laughter:

> *Democritus* ne'r laugh'd so loud
> To see Bauds carted through the crowd,
> Or Funerals with stately Pomp,
> March slowly on in solemn dump;
> As she laugh'd out, until her back
> As well as sides, was like to crack.
> (2:1, ll. 81–86)

Democritean laughter is festive laughter, which Bakhtin defines as a "universal philosophical principle"—laughter that has not yet been reduced to individual mockery and that still retains the "triumphal tones of birth and renewal" (*Rabelais and His World,* 64, 67–70). But except for this one uncontrollable outburst, the tones of festivity are absent in the widow's laughter. Like the popular image of woman in the early fabliaux and in Rabelais's novel, the widow debases; she is the foil to her suitor's limitations. But, according to Bakhtin, there was also a positive aspect to the popular image of woman, and this was lost or, at best, abstracted from its fleshly embodiment in the old image, as that was taken up by later moralistic satire and the comedy of manners: woman was also the principle of birth—not only "the bodily grave of man," the agent of doom for all that is spent and completed, but the "inexhaustible vessel of conception" (*Rabelais and His World*, 240). Butler's widow has been a puzzle to readers, I believe, because she is an unrealized type. She is, as an older critical tradition recognized,[26] modeled upon the emasculating women of Gallic tradition—carnival woman; but she lacks the fecundity and regenerative powers of that "complex and contradictory phenomenon" (*Rabelais and His World*, 240). What we miss in the widow is the essential physicality, "the lower bodily stratum" of the popular comic image of woman. Carnival renewal is therefore quite beyond the widow; she merely debases—and she does that with her mind, not her body.

But by intellectualizing the woman of popular comedy, Butler enlisted the widow as an accomplice in the parodying of carnival forms to satirize the poem's "embodiment" of "Spiritual Carnevall." This is most clearly illustrated by the particular carnival spectacle in which she tempts Hudibras to participate, a whipping. Bakhtin completes the festive "image system" of uncrowning and travesty (through costume change) with what he calls "gay thrashing" (*Rabelais and His World*, 198), the most immediately physical and therefore most strikingly ambivalent of these images: thrashing is both death and regeneration, humiliation and praise, the end of an old life and beginning of a new (*Rabelais and His World*, 205). It is the ritual means by which the uncrowned carnival king is reborn.[27] By daring her knight to suffer whipping, then, the widow casts Hudibras in a mock-carnival in which the bragging knight himself ironically evokes the restorative significance of "gay thrashing"—when, for example, he alludes to the Roman custom of freeing slaves with "a blow" (2:1, l. 236) or to the beating ritual by which a lord in disgrace is "restor'd" to the favor of the Negus (2:1, ll. 239–48). The joke here is that Hudibras's references to the regeneration of the beaten body occur in an argument that is intended by the knight to prove the transcendence of his spirit, but that finally demonstrates the priority of his body. The whipping that the widow tempts him to undergo to prove his claim of physical indifference is the act he refuses to submit to out of consideration for his body. Hudibras is debased, then, if he does or does not submit to the whipping. But he is not regenerated. The carnival dynamic is here turned against itself for the sake of the satire: Butler's carnival clown will never be reborn a king.

The skimmington that follows directly upon the widow's baiting of the knight is another instance of Butler's use of festive form to achieve satirical effect; indeed, for a reading of the poem as carnival, the skimmington, a mock celebration of an inversion of the sexual hierarchy, is a more integral element of the story of Hudibras than the bearbaiting. Unlike the latter, a contest in which the knight actively engaged, the skimmington is a purely mimetic form, the real subjects of which (usually portrayed by substitutes[28]) are unable to do more than suffer the notoriety of their shame. For good reason, then, we might suspect the objectivity of a criticism of the skimmington by one who might otherwise be expected to endorse the censure of men who surrender authority to women. Butler's extraordinary attention to detail in the description of this ritual (the passage has become a *locus classicus* for cultural historians) may be an indication of the distance of his age from an authentic popular tradition—indeed, suggests that the satirist himself may have had to work up the account from secondary sources. But if Butler's contemporary readers needed to be informed of the popular festive significance of the skimmington, Hudibras and Ralpho do not. The knight—who has just been delivered from the stocks by one woman and, before that, been forced to change roles with another— cannot help but see himself as the represented subject of the ritual and attempts to subvert this application in a flurry of classical and Popish irrelevancies: it is "a *Paganish* Invention, / Which *Heathen* Writers often mention" (2:2, ll. 667–68), he insists, "an *Antichristian Opera,* / Much us'd in midnight-times of Popery" (2:2, ll. 769–70).

It is Ralpho again who reveals the carnival significance of the skimmington and, by implication, his uncrowned master's relation to it when he tells Hudibras that "for, all th'*Antiquity* you smatter," the procession

> Is but a *Riding,* us'd of Course,
> When the *Grey Mare's the better Horse.*
> When o're the Breeches greedy *Women*
> Fight, to extend their vast *Dominion.*
> (2:2, ll. 696–700)

The knight, of course, rejects Ralpho's interpretation as an inperti-
nence. It is not defeat, but retreat, he argues, that is the shameful cause
of the skimmington: "to turn *Tayl,* or run away / . . . only unto such,
this Shew / Of *Horns* and *Petticoats* is due" (2:2, ll. 723, 729–30).
Whether or not, then, Hudibras is the intended subject of the skimmington, he will make himself its proper subject when, after a volley of
egg and something "which for good manners / Shall here be nameless"
(2:2, ll. 629–30), he performs that very retreat himself.

In the "Third and Last Part" of *Hudibras,* Butler provides two end-
ings to the carnival satire I have been sketching here. The first of these
(which may well be part of the initial conception of the poem) brings to
a climax the satiric exposure of the Puritan knight in a scene in which
he is tricked into making *"an open, free Confession"* (3:1, l. 1172) of his
hypocrisy. In the "Argument" to canto 1 of part 3 (published almost
fifteen years after part 2), Butler identifies this action with the popular
festive form by which he defined "Spiritual Carnevall" in his prose
observations, that is, a *"Masquerade."* The climactic episode of the
narrative, then, provides corroborative evidence of the importance of
popular festivity in the poem. One may question, however, whether
the masquerade of *Hudibras* functions as carnival spectacle at all, or
simply as satire, since it is introduced not to violate the boundaries of
identity—a violation that is essential to what Bakhtin calls the "gay
relativity" of authentic carnival masquerade (*Rabelais and His World,*
39–40)—but to establish the principle of conformity to self, to reduce
the double self of the spiritual hypocrite to its essential carnality.
Paradoxically, the masquerade is the occasion for Hudibras not to wear,
but to remove a mask. As if to acknowledge this contradiction of
carnival logic, Butler used the word *"Antimasquerade"* in the recapitula-
tion of this scene in the final canto of the poem (3:3, l. 83). Perhaps,
too, he modeled the word on the term *anti-masque,* the word used to
designate the grotesque or melodramatic introductory section of a court
masque.

The antimasque contains the spoken portions of a masque, those
parts reserved for professional players licensed (as elite, dancing
masquers were not) to violate the "congruence of inward and outward
actions";[29] it introduced a world of misrule, accident and vice, "everything," says Stephen Orgel, "that the ideal world of the . . . courtly
main masque, was to overcome and supersede."[30] Butler's masque(rade)
of course travesties this structure since it wants entirely an idealizing
"main masque"; nevertheless, its similarity to the formal model is

suggestive. Variously described as "Pageant," "Ceremony" (3:3, ll. 125, 85), a "treat" and an "entertainment" in the knight's honor, it is the most theatrical episode of the poem, employing costumed and, it must be supposed, rehearsed players, the whole quite literally staged and lighted (3:1, ll. 1317–18) by the widow, who is author (plotter), director and audience of the production. Hudibras's relation to the antimasque(rade), it should be noted, is neither quite that of a participant nor a spectator. Mistaking the fiction for reality, he simply attempts to hide; for him, the masquerade is neither carnival—where there is no distinction between participant and spectator—nor theater, where this distinction is a mutually acknowledged convention.[31]

The masque, Jean-Christophe Agnew writes, never "relinquished its claims of ritual efficacy"; "what the spectator watched he ultimately became" on its "talismanic stage," a transformation normally effected, Stephen Orgel explains, in the revels, the dance between masquers and members of the audience.[32] When the royal spectator joined the revels, he *became* his idealized role in the spectacle, the character of power created for him to fill. Hudibras also may be said to move from the place of the spectator to the place of the spectacle, though the antimasquers must drag him there from "his Redoubt" beneath a table (3:1, l. 1145). But when the hypocrite-knight enters the travestied mimesis of the antimasque(rade), he vacates his character, voids his role; he becomes merely himself, a body he has attempted to disown— or what remains of it, an empty skin or "*Croop,* / Unserviceable with Kicks and Blows," which the tormenting "Spirit Ralpho hors'd . . . like a Sack, / Upon the *Vehicle,* his Back" (3:1, ll. 1560–61, 1571–72). There is little left here of the carnival fat-man, little of the festive mood of popular carnival. The widow's outburst of hearty Democritean laughter has become a satirical snicker; Ralpho later reports to the knight that she "Tee-he'd with derision, / To see them take your Deposition" (3:3, ll. 132–33).

If indeed Butler conceived of the English Commonwealth as a "Spiritual Carnevall"[33] and had by 1660 composed the First (and probably some of the Second) Part of *Hudibras,* he must not only have shared the common joy of most Englishmen at the final dissolution of the Rump Parliament in February of that year, but also have felt some private satisfaction at the form in which popular feeling expressed itself at this historical juncture: a ritual rump-burning—at once a satirical "roast" (or "basting") and a feast, a celebration of the passing of the old times and the coming of the new. Butler offers a vivid account of the event as a supposedly adventitious ending to the long second canto of the "Third and Last Part" of the poem. More important, the passage provides the second conclusion to the carnivalesque satire of *Hudibras*. But the presence in the poem of the Rump (as either political fact or popular joke) need not be regarded as fortuitous. If Wilders's limit-date for the poem's composition is correct,[34] Butler may have been putting the finishing touches to the "First Part" while the rumps were roasting in the streets, and, as his frequent jokes on the "bum" and buttocks of his hero suggest, his association of the carnality of the Puritan saint and the corporal implications of the term "Rump" was probably made quite early.

This association of the knight and the Rump is, of course, a common feature of interpretations of the poem as political satire. "Hudibras is a living rump," says William Horne: the knight's "lower faculties threaten to gain control of his reason, just as the most irrational social element within England has gained control of the body politic"; and Michael Seidel argues that Hudibras's burden of his own buttocks is "the burden of factional monstrosity, the very image of the 'Rump.' "[35] It is not my intention to reverse these views, to try to make Butler an advocate of the "lower faculties" or of "factional monstrosity"; but I do want to take into account the nonsymbolic values of Hudibras's body, the simply physical side of the pun on "Rump," and to notice the immediate relevance of these values in the carnival context of the poem. Butler's parody of excessive figural exegesis in *Hudibras* is itself a recommendation to read "the body" (however sanitized the poem may render it) primarily as *body*. From this point of view, what makes the belly and buttocks of Hudibras and the "rump" of the restored Long Parliament comic monstrosities is the accompanying pretense that the flesh and its appetites and passions do not exist. The knight is a ready target for carnival abuse, then, because he is a hypocrite, one who affects the denial of body in the name of mind and spirit while in fact using these higher faculties to fulfill his carnal interests. The roasting and basting of rumps is yet another carnival abuse of hypocrisy—in this instance, hypocrisy institutionalized.

The carnival significance of the rump-burning episode is first ironically suggested in a Puritan witness's exegesis of the event—mock-exegesis, perhaps,[36] but not, like Hudibras's earlier interpretations of the bearbaiting and the skimmington, dematerializing exegesis. What terrifies the witness is his recognition that the burning rumps represent a physical threat to his own body: " 'tis a miracle, we are not / Already sacrific'd Incarnate," he exclaims (3:2, ll. 1523–24). It is, properly, carnival exegesis: the *"Hieroglyphick Rumps"* represent the seats of power, "the Fundament of all" natural and political bodies; and the "Rump of Man" possesses the secret of renewal and regeneration, the Rabbinical *"Luez"* from which "at the last great Day, / All th'other Members shall . . . / Spring . . ."(3:2, ll. 1615–21). More interesting yet is the final passage of canto 2, which brings into carnival focus two of the poem's recurring motifs, the image of the spurred horse and the buttocks-on-back figure mentioned in the preceding paragraph. As Hudibras's humpback is the unconcealable evidence of his carnality (and the proof, thereby, of his hypocrisy), so the assembled Presbyterians and Independents, put to rout by the advancing mob of demonstrators, recreate the same figure in their panic to escape, compacting themselves into a grotesque melange of bodies, reliteralizing the suppressed physical implications of the Rump metaphor: The Saints, we are told,

> . . . block'd the passage fast,
> And Barricadoed it with *Haunches,*
> Of *outward Men, and Bulks, and Paunches:*
> . . . . . . . . . . . . .
> Still pressing-on, with heavy packs.
> Of one another, on their Backs
> (3:2, ll. 1670–78)

The horse image (which is a complex variation of this figure) made its initial appearance at the end of canto 1, part 1, where the horse is explicitly identified with "a *Common-weal,*" and its rider is probably meant to represent Oliver Cromwell, who, "the more he kick'd and spurr'd, / The less the sullen Jade has stirr'd (1:1, ll. 918–20). Later, in the breathless report of the fearful witness of the rump-burnings in part 3, the Commonwealth-horse is identified exclusively with the "Rabble" which has "Hors'd us [the assembly of Presbyterian and Independent statesmen] on their Backs to show us / A Jadish trick at last, and throw us" (3:2, ll. 1613–14). And, in the final couplet of this canto (3:2, ll. 1689–90), the horse image occurs once more, this time as "a *Tuscan running Horse,*" uncontrolled, riderless (or, to be precise, with a "Jocky-Rider that is all Spurs"). Although the image is used here by the narrator to describe the self-induced panic of the routed assembly-men, it is still the Puritan witness's earlier image of the incorrigible

"Rabble," imagined now in the full career of its achieved liberty. In point of fact, it is a utopian image, an allusion to the riderless horse races held in the Roman Corso at carnival time.[37] Taken together, then, the "sullen Jade" of part 1 and the self-spurred *running Horse* of part 3 define the English Commonwealth in terms of the poem's pervasive opposition of "Spiritual Carnevall" to popular carnival. But there is something terrible about these last scenes of popular festivity—where body obstructs rather than transcends itself and riderless horses whip themselves and one another into frenzy. These are carnival spectacles from the point of view of the passive spectator—of the terrified Puritan who witnesses the rump-burnings and, one supposes, of the once again (or still) alienated Butler who wrote them at the distance of yet another carnival. Reflecting, at some time after 1667, upon the Restoration inversion of Commonwealth hypocrisy, Butler wrote in the "Satyr Upon the Licentious Age of Charles the 2D" that twice men have "turn'd the *World* . . . The wrong Side outward, like a *Jugler's* Pocket,

> Shook out Hypocrisy, as fast and loose,
> As e're the *Dev'l* could teach, or Sinners use,
> And on the other Side at once put in
> As impotent Iniquity, and Sin.[38]

# Chapter Five

# Butler's Prose Characters

Although none of Butler's prose Characters was published in his lifetime, Robert Thyer, who first published 121 of them in *The Genuine Remains* (1759), surmised from the state of the author's manuscripts that some had been prepared for the press. In 1908, A. R. Waller reprinted Thyer's collection along with sixty-six additional Characters which Thyer had also transcribed from Butler's manuscripts. Eleven more have since come to light. Eight of these found their way into some numbers of the *London Magazine* (1825–26), and another ("Schoolmaster") turned up in William Longueville's commonplace book. Two more Characters, "War" and "A Covetous Man" (said to be an early version of "The Miser"), have been uncovered in the holograph British Museum manuscript material by Hugh de Quehen and are published, for the first time as Characters, in his edition of the *Prose Observations*.[1] This brings the total of Butler's Characters to 198, not counting fragments, the largest production of any English writer of the form.

According to Thyer, "most" of the Characters he printed in the *Genuine Remains* had been dated by Butler—"chiefly drawn up," he says, from 1667 to 1669."[2] The dates of only four of the remaining holograph Characters survive, however: "Bankrupt," 6 October 1667; "Horse-Courser" and "Churchwarden," both dated 8 October 1667; and "War," 13 October 1667. By that time, the popularity of Theophrastan Character books—collections of prose sketches of social, psychological, moral, and professional types—had run its course. In its place had come two variants, the historical Character, a verbal portrait of an actual person, published singly or as an illustration within some larger context, and what Benjamin Boyce has named the "polemical" Character, a vigorously biased description of a particular set of religious or political beliefs.[3]

Butler was no doubt familiar with the entire tradition of Character writing (the Theophrastan Greek originals were first translated into Latin by Isaac Casaubon in 1592), for we find traces of all the genre's varieties in his total output. With respect to subject, for instance, many of Butler's Characters exhibit that English combination of a moral portrait with a social type, a development usually credited to the collection published under Sir Thomas Overbury's name, but including specimens since attributed to John Webster, Thomas Dekker, and others. There are in Butler's collection a number of titles suggesting the older portraits of abstract vices ("A Proud Man," "A Debauched Man," "The Luxurious," "A Coward") that Joseph Hall popularized in 1608 in his *Characters of Vertues and Vices*, the earliest English imitation of Theophrastus. But in addition to the Character of "An Hypocrite," for example, Butler also gives us "An Hypocritical Nonconformist," the older moral interest existing here (as also in "A Degenerate Noble," "A Huffing Courtier," and "A Corrupt Judge") principally for the sake of presenting an existing social type; moreover, it is clear that Butler regards the "Hypocrite" not purely as a moral type (compare Joseph Hall's more Theophrastan counterpart), but as an ecclesiastical figure. This interest in social analysis is shown even more clearly by the thoroughness with which Butler surveys human occupations, from the highest professions (legal, religious, medical, and academic) to the lowest trades. Within these general categories, he makes even further distinctions, often defining an institutional hierarchy of professional culpability. The legal types, for example, rise from the lowly "Knight of the Post" and "Justice of the Peace," through the "Pettifogger" and "Lawyer," to the "Alderman" and "Judge"; we may also wish to find a place within this hierarchy for the peripheral legal figures of the "Catchpole," "Constable," "Jailor," and "Jurer," bearing in mind, however, that the degree of unethical behavior increases proportionately with rank.

The historical Character, or, as David Nichol Smith suggests, the deliberate blending of historical portrait and Theophrastan Character,[4] is represented by Butler's "A Duke of Bucks," the poet's punning allusion to his noble employer, George Villiers, Duke of Buckingham, a type of perversion in human nature. With lese certainty, we may also include in this class "An Haranguer" (William Prynne?), "An Hermetic Philosopher" (Thomas Vaughn?), and "A Small Poet" (Edward Benlowes?). Finally, in his portraits of ideological and religious types (in "A Republican," "A Fifth-Monarchy Man," and "A Latitudinarian," for instance), and in his occasional extension of Characters to essay length ("A Modern Politician" runs to over seven thousand five hundred words) we have examples of the late polemical Character. Butler's close relation to the whole Character tradition is also indicated by his borrowings from some of the earlier practitioners of the form, particularly from specimens in John Earle's *Microcosmography* (1628, 1633) and from the polemical pieces of Richard Flecknoe and John Cleveland.[5] Butler's "Clown [or Rustic], for example—one who "manures the Earth like a Dung-hill, but lets himself lye Fallow" (131)—is clearly descended from Earle's "Plain Country Fellow," who "manures his ground wel, but lets himself lie fallow and untill'd." From Cleveland's (Character of a Diurnal-Maker" (1647), Butler drew such details as the "Curious Man's" "iron Chain . . . about the Neck of a Flea" and his "Iliads in a Nut-shell" (105), the "Fanatic's" "Portugese Horses" (96), and the "Melancholy Man's" "falling Sickness" (97–98).

Of the emergence of the Overburian Character, the development of which we have been following in terms of Butler's production, W. J. Paylor observes that "the writer of the *Overburian Character* is not primarily interested in the texture of one particular fault out of which a man is neatly cut to the pattern of a dissembler or a flatterer. His criticism is centered upon the varied vices and mannerisms of the social types around him, and his portraits are influenced in their composition more by contemporary drama, satire, and pamphlets, wherein these figures abound, than by classical Character."[6] The author of such Characters, we might say, had become a social scientist in his approach to behavior, less interested in demonstrating the existence of universals in human nature than in recording the actual manners of certain classes of individuals. This change in view would have suited perfectly Butler's own empirical turn of mind. But there is an important difference between Butler's Characters of social analysis (and his polemical Characters) and those of his contemporaries and Overburian predecessors. Butler's method is ultimately reductive. Although he appears to be chiefly interested in describing a multiplicity of types, of treating every nameable variety of human society, what his Characters in fact reveal is the persistence of one or two motives of folly or villainy inherent in almost every variety of human nature. Specifically, these motivations are man's need to deceive himself and his ingenuity in the use of reason to devise means of deceiving others. For all their apparent interest in contemporary manners, Butler's Characters are firmly rooted in the moral assumptions of their author.

Taken as a body, then, Butler's Characters appear to present a conflict of intention in the author: on the one hand, they reveal the essential, hidden perversity of human nature (Butler has left us no Character of a virtuous subject); on the other, they depict the infinite variety through which that perversity manifests itself. Butler seems compelled to name these varieties or "professions," to undo the conspiracy of silence in our social institutions that he alludes to in his Character of "A Cheat": "all the greater Sort of Cheats being allowed by Authority, have lost their Names (as *Judges,* when they are called to the Bench, are no more stiled *Lawyers*) and left the title to the meaner only, and the unallowed" (171). Butler is therefore also interested in what he terms the "Callings," the inherent aptitudes or ruling passions of his subjects. Specifically, he focuses upon the discrepancy between "calling" and "profession," for this difference constitutes the satiric situation of his Characters. The Character of "A Cheat," for example, makes clear the close interdependence that Butler finds among his subjects: the Cheat "is a Freeman of all Trades, and all Trades of his," it begins (170); and later: "He can do no Feats without the cooperating Assistance of the Chowse [Gull], whose Credulity commonly meets the Imposter half Way, otherwise nothing is done; for all the Craft is not in the Catching (as the Proverb says) but the better half at least in being catched" (171). Often, two Characters represent merely two views of the same deception, as "A Popish Priest" and "A Proselite," "A Lawyer" and "A Litigious Man," "A Mountebank" and "A Medicine-Taker." Butler is able to name the character even of a subject that has no "calling," a characterless-Character, as it were. "A Cully," or Dupe—a nonentity himself—is described entirely in terms of the actions of those who work upon him: he "is a gibbet for all manner of cheats and rogues to hang upon; a Bridewel [a prison], where pickpockets and rooks are set on work and kept . . . Gamesters knap him with a whore . . . and rooks build in him like a tree" (266).

Other Characters illustrate Butler's conviction that all extremes are ultimately identities—as "A Popish Priest" and "A [Puritan] Fanatic," or "A Philosopher" and "A Mathematician" (the mathematician beginning "in Nonsense . . . ends in Sense, and the other [the philosopher] quite contrary begins in Sense and ends in Nonsense" [119]). Of particular interest in this connection are the unexpected relationships that Butler reveals as existing between the subjects of quite different Characters, professional disparities that are wittily brought into focus as a single image. Thus, "An Hermetic Philosopher . . . is a Kind of Hector in Learning, that thinks to maintain himself in Reputation by picking Quarrels with his gentle Readers" (139); "A Modern Critic" is "a Mountebank, that is always quacking of the infirm and diseased

Parts of Books, to shew his Skill" (183); the alcohol in a "Sot" is like the inner light of a Quaker (162); "A Virtuoso" is compared to (of all things) a "Country-gentleman" (compare Butler's "Bumpkin or Country Squire" [74]): as the squires "talk of Dogs to those that hate Hunting, because they love it themselves; so will he of his Arts and Sciences to those that neither know, nor care to know any Thing of them" (122).

This practice of interchanging character types provided Butler with a special rhetoric, a secondary language of "professions" designed to articulate the especially elusive "callings," and furthermore enabling him to reuse apt witticisms without the effect of repetition. The "Republican," for example, "is a civil Fanatic . . . and as all Fanatics cheat themselves with Words, mistaking them for Things; so does he with the false Sense of Liberty" (55). The "Virtuoso" "differs from a Pedant, as *Things* do from *Words;* for he uses the same Affectation in his Operations and Experiments, as the other does in Language" (122). Butler's metaphorical vehicles are self-generating, spreading like ripples in wider, more inclusive rings: "A Pimp Is a *Solicitor* of Love, a Whore's *Broker, Procurator* of the most serene Commonwealth of Sinners, and *Agent* for the Flesh and the Devil" (235—italics added). Such figures, demonstrating the essential unity of the various forms of human folly and villainy, suggest that Butler's penchant for analogy—"If ever a man was haunted by 'the demon of analogy,' it was he," writes Ian Jack[7]—was in fact the natural consequence of his peculiar view of the nature of life. John Wilders and Hugh de Quehen see this instinct for analogy as evidence of Butler's commitment to an older, analogical worldview that celebrated universal order.[8] Would it not be more reasonable, though, to understand the analogical language of the Characters as a burlesque of that view of order, or to find the source of this language in that paradox we noticed in chapter 2: that, whereas the singleness of truth is the most difficult achievement in the world, the devising of passable alternatives to truth (that is, falsehoods) is the easiest. Falsehood, Butler observed in the prose observations, "has change of faces and every one proof against all impression" (24:3). Like a modern psychologist, he, too, recognized that human beings assume roles for social or personal reasons; but he regarded this phenomenon as a cause for laughter or rebuke, rather than for understanding or sympathy. To Butler, the danger of such behavior lay not in any violation of individual integrity (though, of course, the deceived is always at the mercy of the deceiver), but in the undermining of any surviving trace of order in human society. The man who assumes the name, but not the virtues, of learning, piety, nobility, or justice creates a confusion that makes these virtues—rare enough to begin with—all the more inaccessible.

In pointing out this deception, Butler's Characters seem to make only a negative claim to truth: Justice is *not* this magistrate or that attorney, they say; this "Huffing Courtier" is *not* a picture of nobility. Nevertheless, a positive value shines through this apparently destructive outlook; for, if we are brought to see that Justice is merely a judge's "profession," it is likely that we shall be on our guard in the future against his true "calling," amassing wealth. "As other mens harmes make us cautious, so the Miscarriages of others may make us wise," Butler remarked in the prose observations. "He that see's another in a wrong way, is so much nearer to the right himself" (9:5).

"The Generall Temper of Mankind," Butler observed, "is nothing but a Mixture of Cheat and Folly" (11:2). Let us, therefore, consider his Characters as portraits of deceivers and the victims of deception (their own or another's). The victims, Butler's fools, we have noticed earlier, misunderstand their true natures because they either lack reason (the madmen and proper or "natural" fools) or because they misuse it (the ignorant or "artificial" fools); and, as a consequence of both causes, they bear a closer resemblance to animals or machines than to men. I have explained the general category of folly using Butler's assertion that "Men without Reason [and men who misuse it] . . . fall short of that which give's them their Being . . ." (68:3). Such a man, we read in the Character of "A Fool," is "not actuated by any inward principle of his own, but by something without him, like an engine; for he is nothing, but as he is wound up, and set a going by others" (275)—by others, or by the fluctuating pressures of his own passions or "humours": but in neither case does he remain himself. The result, viewed from the outside, is usually ridiculous: the "Affected [Man]," for example, "is a Piece of Clockwork, that moves only as it is wound up and set, and not like a voluntary Agent" (237); and the "Sot" "has washed down his soul and pist it out . . . has swallowed his Humanity and drunk himself into a Beast, as if he had pledged *Madam Circe*. . . . He governs all his Actions by the Drink within him . . . [and having] a different humour for every Nick his Drink rises to . . . proceeds from Ribaldry to Bawdery to Politics, Religion, and Quarreling . . ." (162–63). Or here is the "Fantastic," the seventeenth-century dandy who exists merely to embody the changing modes of fashion: "His Brain is like Quicksilver, apt to receive any Impression, but retain none. . . . He is a Cormorant, that . . . devours every Thing greedily, but it runs through him immediately" (96). This wild instability of character, which is typical of natural folly or madness, contrasts, as we shall see, with the obsessive behavior exhibited in many types of artificial folly.

Except, perhaps, for those natural fools who seem compelled to be other than themselves (the "Affected [Man]," the "Sot," and the "Fantastic"), playing a role is presented as, generally, a pleasurable experience; and this pleasure bears out the truth of Butler's belief that men are happiest when devising tricks that keep them from thinking about their own miseries and weaknesses—happiness as "a perpetual Possession of being well Deceived," in Swift's later formulation. It is only to the objective observer that unnatural behavior is painful, for it appears to him as destructive to individual integrity as innovation is to national integrity. In the Character of the "Affected [Man]," Butler conveys this view, the sheer difficulty of the unnatural, through the use of an analogy of organic growth:

All his Affections are forced and stolen from others, and though they become some particular Persons where they grow naturally, as a Flower does on its Stalk, he thinks they will do so by him, when they are pulled and dead. He puts Words and Language out of its ordinary Pace, and breaks it to his own Fancy, which makes it go so uneasy in a Shuffle, which it has not been used to. He delivers himself in a forced Way like one that sings with a feigned Voice beyond his natural Compass.

(193)

This behavior, of course, is a form of social affectation, adopting the clothes and mannerisms of a social station higher than one's own. More interesting to Butler was what we might call professional affectation, the dabbling in some rather prestigious occupation for which one has no aptitude. But the motivation for both forms of pretense is identical: "All the Business of this World is but *Diversion*," the devising of "tricks" by which men manage to ignore their own shortcomings (2:1). Even the most humble occupation should be self-fulfilling, and, to the degree that it is, its product has a value. But men literally lose themselves in their occupations, with the result that their labors are fruitless. Butler's Character of "An Officer" (no more precise title will fit him) is the clearest statement of the idea: "Nature meant him for a man, but his office intervening put her out, and made him another thing; and as he loses his name in his authority, so he does his nature.

The most predominant part in him is that in which he is something beside himself" (294).

The Character of "An Officer" explains the fatal attraction of those persuits that Pope later satirized as "dullness," and that Butler analyzed more particularly in the Characters of "A Curious Man," "A Virtuoso," "An Hermetic Philosopher," and "A Pedant." Before becoming "An Officer," we read, the subject "was nothing of himself, but had a great ambition to be something, and so got an office, which he stands more upon than if he had been more of himself; for having no intrinsic value he has nothing to trust to but the stamp that is set upon him, and so is necessitated to make as much of that as he can" (295). Pedantry in any profession justifies itself in the same way. Butler's "Pedant" happens to be a physician, but could be a member of any profession: "he gives his Patients sound hard words for their Money, as cheap as he can afford; for they cost him Money and Study too, before he came by them, and he has Reason to make as much of them as he can" (188). The *little* that such pretenders make much of is their capacity to engage in "the ordinary Bus'nes, and Drudgery of the world" (18:2), the office for which nature originally designed them, endowing them with qualities like patience and industriousness, which then become comically inappropriate to the roles they tend to assume, and cause them to succeed only in perverting their usefulness in the world. Created for slavery, such men turn whatever occupation they pretend to into drudgery. Thus the "Virtuoso," or dilettante, having "nothing of Nature but an Inclination . . . strives to improve [it] with Industry," which would itself be admirable "if it did not attempt [only] the greatest Difficulties . . . for he commonly slights any Thing that is plain and easy . . . and bends all his Forces against the hardest and most improbable" (122).

It is only a step from such comic forms of self-delusion (costing the pretender only an occasional embarrassment) to much more troublesome forms of deception. In fact, the only thing preventing our taking a sterner view of the fools whom we have thus far considered is Butler's assurance of their total innocence or irrationality. But the moment the "Virtuoso" (for instance) embarks upon an impossible pursuit—because it is impossible and because it permits him to say or do whatever he pleases (since no man may say he is wrong)—he deceives not only himself (or more likely not himself at all), but another. We then have what Butler (adopting the new scientific interest in motion to explain the processes of deception) called the "Mechanics of Cheat" and the "mathematical Magic of Imposture" (162), the science of which he is perhaps the most perceptive analyst in English.

We might, in fact, regard Butler's Characters as a much more comprehensive and much more subtle Restoration version of the old Elizabethan coney-catching books, those collections of admonitory fictions exposing the techniques of thieves and confidence men. How does "A Ranter," one of a wild sect of religious libertines who openly defamed the scriptures, the church, and all its conventions, practice deception? Or in what sense can the charge of deception be levelled at "A Latitudinarian," a seventeenth-century church liberal who was all for dissolving those narrow denominational differences that offered a sort of orthodox sanction for religious hypocrisy? Butler's answers to such questions in the Characters illustrate his extraordinary interest in knavery as a conscious mental process (*signification,* we would call it today), an interest that recognized that appearances and statements exert predictable and adaptable forces. For Butler, deception was a problem in mechanics, not semiotics. The "Knave" is "an Engineer of Treachery, Fraud, and Perfidiousness," who knows "how to manage Matters of great Weight with very little Force, by the Advantage of his trepanning Screws" (214). Butler's portraits of knavery trace the progress of this science. The "Ranter," for example, has "found out by a very strange Way of new Light, how to transform all the *Devils* into *Angels of Light*" (106). When a society as sophisticated as Restoration England has come to recognize saintliness as the mask of true wickedness, may not an unsaintly manner carry the force of virtue? In his "Satyr upon the Licentious Age of Charles the 2D," Butler explained the change from Commonwealth to Restoration mores in just this way:

> For those, who heretofore sought private Holes,
> Securely in the Dark to damn their Souls,
> Wore Vizards of Hypocrisy, to steal
> And slink away, in Masquerade, to *Hell,*
> Now bring their Crimes into the open *Sun,*
> For all Mankind to gaze their worst upon.
> (*Satires,* 11. 35–40)

Thus the "Ranter" "puts off the *old Man,* but puts it on again upon the *new one.* . . . He is but an *Hypocrite* turned the wrong Side outward; for, as the one wears his Vices within, and the other without, so when they are counter-changed the *Ranter* becomes an *Hypocrite,* and the *Hypocrite* an able *Ranter*" (106–7). On the other hand, the "Latitudinarian" is simply "a Kind of modest Ranter" (118): he maintains that "*Christian* Liberty and *natural* Liberty may very well consist together"; and, in the event of a conflict between the two, he is prepared to give the latter ("being of the elder House") the "Precedency."

Often the line between a subject's ignorance of his motivations and his deliberate self-misrepresentation is difficult to draw. Butler's "Fanatic," for example, seems willing to endure persecution in order to conceal his unwillingness to channel his energies toward a more effective end. "He is all for suffering for Religion, but nothing for acting; for he accounts *good Works* no better than Encroachments upon the Merits of *free believing . . .*" (127). Yet this Character begins with Butler's observation that "the *Fanatics* of out times are mad with too little [learning]" (126); and Butler concludes by calling him "a Puppet Saint" whose "Ignorance is the dull leaden Weight that puts all his Parts in Motion" (128). Although there is remarkable logical consistency of opinion in the Characters, it is difficult to generalize from them to what could confidently be regarded as Butler's attitude toward his subjects. If his view of the "Fanatic" seems strangely ambivalent, his judgments upon similar faults in the "Sceptic" and the "Zealot" (a second version of the (Fanatic)) are not: in "undervaluing that, which he cannot attain to," the "Sceptic" would make his Necessity appear a Virtue . . ." (165); and of the "Zealot" we are told "his Zeal is never so vehement, as when it concurs with his Interest. . . . He is very severe to other Men's Sins, that his own may pass unsuspected . . ." (231).

We know from a statement in his notebook that Butler, like Dante, took a graver view of fraud than of violence: "a Cheat is worse than a Thiefe," he wrote; for the former "do's not only Rob a man of his Goodes (as a thiefe do's) but his Reputation also, and makes him Combine and take Part against himself: Steale's and convey's him, out of his Reason, and Senses . . ." (58:4). In general, the Characters can be read as a demonstration of this Aristotelian view of wrongdoing. Nevertheless, Butler's moral bias should not allow us to forget his relationship to the Overburian writers and, in particular, to their conversion of the traditional moral Character into an occasion for witty improvisation. Butler continued this tradition by employing the Character as an intellectual exercise, a "diversion," according to Earl Miner,[9] rather than a form of moral exhortation—organizing large parts of a particular portrait around a central image, creating an entire sketch out of contrasting conceits, or testing the limits of ironic perspective.

Butler would have taken little satisfaction as an artist in repeating, for example, the hackneyed anti-Catholic prejudices that he no doubt shared as an English Protestant. He therefore begins his Character of "A Popish Priest" by taking for granted certain contemporary assumptions about the subject—about the priest's "profession." Specifically, he assumes that every man, at least, knows that the Catholic priest's chief duty in England is to infiltrate the family in order to proselytize its women, and so "his Profession is to disguise himself, which he does in Sheep's-Cloathing, that is, a Lay Habit" (100). There is, in other words, no question about the essentially deceptive nature of priesthood; nor is there, for once, any mystery about the discrepancy between the subject's "profession" and his true "calling." Or is there? The "great Question," Butler goes on to say, is whether the "Sheep's-Cloathing" of the priest covers a "Wolf, a Thief, or a Shepherd." Interestingly, in Milton's *Lycidas,* the thief and the wolf are combined in a figure that blurs the distinction between Anglican and Roman clergy: while the Christian flocks "rot inwardly" in the care of Episcopacy, the idle and greedy clergymen "for their bellies' sake, / Creep and intrude and climb into the fold," while "the grim wolf [understood as a Catholic] with privy paw / Daily devours apace, and nothing said." The good shepherd, Lycidas, or those who weep for him, remain to represent the reformed churches. The flocks in Butler's character are also "rotten"—though "with Hypocrisy"—and the Popish priest is clearly a thief: "only this is certain, that he had rather have one Sheep out of another Man's fold, than two out of his own." But he is more a thieving shepherd than a wolf: he "keeps his Flock always in Hurdles . . . [and] . . . he tars their Consciences with Confession and Penance, but always keeps the Wool, that he pulls from the Sore, to himself" (100). Butler makes no distinction between the priest and Milton's shepherd: "He gathers his Church as Fanatics do." The reader may answer the "great Question" as he pleases; the author, we might believe, considered it a purely rhetorical one. For Butler, this Character was primarily a form of witty play, testing the validity of the cliché.

Often Butler's play is pure invention, the exercise of the imagination upon only one or two features of the subject. In the following allusions to the "Anabaptist's" affinity for water, for example, we notice how self-contained—how much a part of the witty allusions themselves—is the polemical force of the Character:

[He is] a Water-saint, that like a Crocodile, sees clearly in the Water, but dully on Land.

[He lives] in two Elements like a Goose.

He is contrary to a Fisher of Men; for instead of pulling them out of the water, he dips them in it.

He is a Landerer of Souls, and tries them, as Men do Witches, by Water, He dips them all under Water, but their Hands, which he holds them up by— those do still continue *Pagan*.

His dipping makes him more obstinate and stiff in his Opinions, like a Piece of hot Iron, that grows hard by being quenched in cold Water.

He does not like the use of Water in his Baptism, as it falls from Heaven in Drops, but as it runs out of the Bowels of the Earth, or stands putrefying in a dirty Pond.

He chuses the coldest Time in the Year to be dipped in, to shew the Heat of his Zeal, and this renders him the more obstinate.

His Church is under the watry Government of the Moon, when she was in *Aquarius*.

He finds out Sloughs and Ditches, that are aptest for launching of an Anabaptist; for he does not christen, but launch his Vessel.

(214–17)

The same procedure is employed in the Characters of "A Huffing Courtier," who is defined in terms of clothing, and of "An Haranguer," which was probably inspired by William Prynne, the Puritan pamphleteer whose libelous tongue cost him both ears in the pillory. Throughout "An Haranguer" Butler plays upon both details ("His Ears have catched the Itch of his Tongue"), and the result is something closer to caricature than portraiture.

I suspect that Butler composed such pieces at great speed, dashing off the images as they came, with one suggesting another. The "Horse-Courser" and the "Churchwarden," we know, were composed on the same day, an association that defies explanation until we reach the final sentence of the "Horse-Courser," who, like a Puritan "Saint," is "a strict observer of Saints Days," when fairs were held, and "where all Sorts of Trades are most used; and always where a Saint has a Fair he has a Church too" (244–45). Butler paid little attention to repetition, sequence, or consistency ("A Rabble," for example, is described as a flock of sheep, a herd of swine, and the "most savage Beast in the whole World" [197–98]); he cared only whether he pressed his imagination to its limit and thoroughly exhausted it on a subject. Rather than expunge or revise, Butler used superfluous imagery to prime his imagination on some new aspect of the subject.

The various imperfections in the Character of "An Undeserving Favourite" (206–9) permit us to form some idea of his working method. Because a "favorite" is literally defined by the favors he receives from his king, Butler's chief emphasis in this Character is upon the contrast between these favors and the undeservingness of the subject. Accordingly, the opening clause defines the type as a coin, but one of "base Metal," a counterfeit, and its sole authenticity is the impression of the king's face that it bears: "An Undeserving Favourite / Is a Piece of base Metal with the King's Stamp upon it"—adding, as if at the suggestion of the color of the base metal or the shape of the coin, this appositive: "[he is] a Fog raised by the Sun, to obscure his own Brightness." This implied concern for the moral reputation of the king ("the Sun") is uncharacteristic of Butler, so much so that we wonder if he has not failed to make his intended point. A similar difficulty appears in the next sentence. "He came to Preferment by unworthy Offices, like one that rises with his Bum forwards, which the Rabble hold to be fortunate." Again the point is obscure; but, rather than delete or revise it, Butler makes another attempt to state it more clearly: "He got up to Preferment on the wrong Side, and sits as untoward in it." And then, as if still unsatisfied with his expression of the idea, he gives us yet another explanation. The favorite is not confortable in his seat of favor; since he does not deserve his place, he does not become it. Based upon something other than worth, his elevation is merely superficial; it fails to distinguish him above his peers: "He is raised rather above himself than others," Butler writes, "or as base Metals are by the Test of Lead, while Gold and Silver continue still unmoved." Though the last figure picks up the metal imagery of the counterfeit coin, we might well feel that "the Test of Lead" is somewhat incorrectly applied in this context since heavy or "base Metals" would be precipitated rather than "raised" from mixtures containing gold or silver (as Butler more nearly suggests with the same figure in the Character of "An Ignorant Man" [282]).

But this figure may also have brought to a more conscious level in Butler's mind several other notions only faintly suggested thus far in the Character. One of these is the juxtaposition, from the very first sentence, of images suggesting both sinking and rising. It is of course in the nature of a favorite to rise, and we may suppose too that he is *light* insofar as he lacks substantial value; but the type is also, for Butler, essentially heavy, dull, leaden, endowed with the qualities of ignorance rather than with intelligence and wit. This paradoxical nature of the favorite now emerges in the alchemical figure as an actual confusion in the author's mind. Furthermore, the figure suggests a new focus of interest in the subject. In order to show that the undeserving favorite is a counterfeit creation, Butler observes that "he is raised rather above himself than others" (207). Although this statement indicates that undeserved favoritism does not alter the essential nature of the favored, it also suggests that it has no effect upon the unfavored, an implication that Butler, as a case of unrecognized merit himself, would probably have rejected. In describing metaphorically the relative effect of favors, Butler suggests, however, the essential injustice of the situation: "Gold and Silver continue still unmoved"—that is, true worth goes unrecognized. We may see now that Butler seems to have been moving toward this idea from the very beginning (we notice, for instance, the increasingly distinct echoes of Shakespeare's thirty-second sonnet); but we only gradually became conscious of it. Not until the fifth sentence is it fully articulated: "He is born like a Cloud on the Air of the Prince's Favour, and keeps his Light from the rest of his People" (207).

Butler's range of metaphorical reference in the Characters is much wider than the preceding passage from "An Undeserving Favourite" indicates. Indeed, it is difficult to think of a field of learning, an activity, or a human experience that does not contribute some image or allusion to his Characters. Much of this material is learned in nature, the product of reading, study, or attention to the complex affairs of contemporary politics, religion, and philosophy. The portrait of "A Fifth-Monarchy-Man," for instance, includes references to Perkin Warbec and Lambert Simnel, political pretenders of earlier English history; the Anabaptist leader, John of Leyden; Romulus, one of the legendary founders of Rome; the abortive insurrection and punishment of Thomas Venner and his Fifth-Monarchy-Men (1660–61); the fairy-land monarchy of King Oberon; Aeneas's visions of the Roman Empire; Mahommed; and King Arthur. Among the philosophers mentioned in the Characters, we find such expected names as Plato, Aristotle, Hobbes, Descartes, Bacon, and More, as well as a number of lesser-known writers on more esoteric branches of the subject, such as Agrippa, Cardon, Charlton, Raymond Lully, Conrad Gesner, Jacob Boehme, and Alexander Ross.

Butler may employ a scholastic distinction in a secular context—like that which compares the conversation of "An Amorist" to the intuition of an angel (108)—or draw upon recent scientific investigation to develop a remark on religion or morality, as when he observes that ritual increases the force of religion in the Catholic much as a magnet draws a greater weight through a piece of iron (104), or compares the Sot's way of renewing his childhood with "the *Virtuoso's* Way of making old Dogs young again," that is, by transfusion (161–62). Even Butler's puns tend to be learned—typographical, like the identification of the "Cuckhold's" head with Pythagoras's letter (both are "troubled with a forked Distinction" [210]); etymological, like the "Undeserving Favourite's *honor*" (it is to be understood in its "original Sense . . . which among the Ancients (*Gellius* says) signified Injury" [208]); or grammatical ("A Pimp" is "a Conjunction copulative, that joins different Cases, Genders, and Persons" [237]). Scriptural allusions (though rather common ones) are frequent, as are also references to the Greek classics and the Roman satirists. But, outside of an obviously literary subject like "A Small Poet," allusions to later literary figures are rare. In the last-named Character, Butler refers to Ben Jonson and Edward Benlowes, the emblem poets, William Prynne, and perhaps Sir William Davenant. Elsewhere, the important French critic Julius Scaliger is several times mentioned, and there are references to Sylvester's translation of Du Bartas, to Chaucer's pilgrims, and to occasional recollections of characters from the plays of Jonson, Marlowe, and Shakespeare.

In marked contrast to this learned material are the allusions to popular legend, fable, and proverb, the imagery of everyday life, and commonsense truth that Butler uses in the Characters. Some of this material may have been recalled from his rural youth and early career at various country estates: glimpses of the wretched roads of the North Country, which appear as an analogy for the tiresome discourse of the "Tedious Man" (173), references to rustic drinking customs (240), and to the special knowledge of farmers, hunters, and fishermen (137, 138, 241, 242). Here, too, is the expertise of popular games—bowls, dice, tennis, *L'Ombre,* and "Inn and Inn"—reference to the forms of popular festivity, and the sights and sounds of the city: the "link-boy" who lights the dark ways (a metaphor for the self-illuminated Quaker [200]); the watchman with his blunt bill speciously "chalk'd" to appear sharp (an analogy of false wit); street names like "Ram-alley" (317) and "Lewkner's Lane" (236); and shop-signs like the "Turks Head," where Harrington's Rota Club met (258), and the vintner's "bush" (217).

For the modern reader, this witty application of the commonplace is probably the most memorable feature of Butler's Characters: the "Haranguer's" tongue, always in motion, though to little purpose, is "like a Barber's Scissors, which are always snipping, as well when they do not cut, as when they do" (99). The clothes-conscious "fantastic," "sure to be earliest in the Fashion, lays out for it like the first Pease and Cherries" (96); on the other hand, the "Knave" "grows rich by the Ruin of his Neighbors, like Grass in the Streets in a great Sickness" (214). One of the few generalizations we can make about such figures—aside from the obvious fact that each presents a fresh impression of Butler's actual world—is that they tend to be one-dimensional: they are merely witty illustrations rather than expressions of insight. True, the image of a luxuriant growth of grass in the street of a plague-infested city is actually quite complex; it may express desertedness, the triumph of the natural over the artificial, or the irrepressibility of the life force. For Butler, however, the value of the image is drastically restricted: he means only that the Knave and the grass are alike in that both flourish at the expense of men. Butler's figures collapse under any greater interpretive pressure. They are to be enjoyed simply as unexpected similitudes, wondered at, perhaps, for their perspicuity, but then dropped for the next in turn; and since the peripheral overtones of these images are nonfunctional, we find little sense of poetic coherence in the Characters. Unity is a feature not of individual Characters, but of the entire collection and is due chiefly to Butler's tendency to repeat images (animals, machinery, clothes). The significant patterns emerge only in broad pespective. Man is a beast—or worse—the Characters say collectively; or man, the rational animal, is a flattering fiction—in reality, he is an automaton; or men are never what they appear to be—all practice some form of deception. These images, and their implications in Butler's thought have been mentioned in earlier chapters. But one other class of repeated imagery may yet be mentioned, that of buying and selling, the making and spending of money, and the production and consumption of commodities.

In many cases, of course, the language and imagery of commerce is called for by the middle-class subjects of the Characters ("A Shop-keeper," "A Vintner," "A Banker"), and Butler is quite adept at employing the special vocabularies of the professions and trades he describes. But I am thinking now of commerce as a metaphor: the "Small Poet" as "Haberdasher . . . with a very small Stock, and no Credit" (82); the "Lawyer" as "Retailer of Justice, that uses false Lights, false Weights, and false Measures" (111); and the "Astrologer" as "Retailer of Destiny, and petty Chapman to the Planets" (110). It is probably a mistake to take such imagery too seriously, or to suggest, as Norma Bentley does, that Butler aspired to membership in the leisure class[10] and hence was contemptuous of the middle class he wished to, but could not, rise above. Indeed, there is a touch of this sentiment in his Character of "A Shopkeeper": "Country Gentlemen," he wrote, "always design the least hopeful of their Children to Trades, and out of that Stock the City is supplied with that sottish Ignorance, which we see it perpetually abound with" (199). It is also true that the middle-class moneymakers of Butler's day were usually Puritans, and of course Butler was critical of the Puritans. But his criticism was directed at the spiritual pretenses of Puritanism, not at its economic philosophy—or, indirectly, at the latter only if it revealed pretense,[11] as in this passage from the long polemical Character of "A Hypocritical Nonconformist":

The Wealth of his Party . . . is no mean Motive to enflame his Zeal, and encourage him to use the Means, and provoke all Dangers, where such large Returns may infallibly be expected. . . . For so many and great have been the Advantages of this thriving Persecution, that the Constancy and Blood of the primitive Martyrs did not propagate the Church more, than the Money and good Creatures earned by these profitable Sufferings have done the Discipline of the modern Brethren.

(46)

The brand of commerce was for Butler not a social, but an ethical, stigma. "Many excellent Persons have been born and lived in the City," he says in the Character of "A City-Wit," but "there are very few such that have been bred there, though they come from all Parts and Families of the Nation; for Wit is not the Practice of the Place and a London Student is like an *University* Merchant" (226). Butler's Characters suggest that the men of commerce were themselves aware of what they had done to trade. The "Shopkeeper," for example cannot call his occupation a "profession," and he is ashamed to regard it as a "calling": he speaks of it, therefore, as a *"Mystery"*; Butler adds, however, that "rightly interpreted [this mystery] signifies only this—That as all *Turks* are Tradesmen, even so all Tradesmen are Turks" (199).

## Chapter Six
# The Vogue of *Hudibras:* Conclusion

Because Butler published little in his lifetime and acknowledged only a portion of that, an assessment of his significance must, in large part, be an account of the popularity and influence of *Hudibras* and its satiric methods. Butler's reputation as a thinker—an aspect of his work that has interested me in this study—has grown slowly, governed, as it has been, by the gradual publication of his notebook materials. As for his Characters, which would have made a real contribution to the rhetoric of prose satire, their publication in 1759 came at a time when the form had already become a historical curiosity and when satire itself had fallen into decline. But the voice of *Hudibras,* or at least something recognizable as an impersonation of that voice, remained as a very audible echo in satiric verse throughout the Restoration and the following century. Jonathan Swift's "You, like some acute Philosopher, / Ev'ry Fault have drawn a Gloss over," from an "Epistle to a Lady," was obviously meant to recall Butler's "There was an ancient sage *Philosopher,* / That had read *Alexander Ross* over," from the beginning of the second canto of *Hudibras,* and Lord Byron's "Carelessly I sing, / But Phoebus lends me now and then a string, / With which I still can harp, and carp, and fiddle, / . . . But now I choose to break off in the middle," from his much later *Don Juan,* recalls the "argument" of the initial canto of Butler's poem. Borrowed rhymes and phrases do not, however, constitute imitation, and although Swift and Byron found certain metrical tricks (and, in the case of the former, a preemption of some of his own best thoughts) in Butler, each was himself an original. The great vogue of Hudibrastic imitation appears in a much less distinguished roster of anonymous hacks, second-rate poetasters, and novices who hoped to gain the public's attention by reworking the vein of the most popular poem of the Restoration.

Perhaps the most commonly imitated feature of *Hudibras* is its rough octosyllabic meter, the doggerel Hudibrastic couplet. It is, of course, impossible to establish a precedent for Butler's practice of this form.

Milton employed tetrameter couplets in *L'Allegro* and *Il Penseroso;* Andrew Marvell used them in "The Garden" and "To His Coy Mistress"; and their value as a vehicle for all sorts of hit-and-run satiric attacks must have extended backwards through broadside ballads and lampoons to the Middle Ages. Butler made something new of this form, however, as the author of the anonymous imitation entitled *Pendragon; or the Carpet Knight* explained in 1698: *Hudibras* "stands upon Four Feet," he wrote, "but its Liberties and Privileges are unbounded; and those Four Feet are, I think, by no means obliged to be but Eight Syllables; for in place of the Last, it is a part of its Excellency some times to have Two, Three, or Four Syllables (like so many Claws) crowded into the Time of One Foot. The Duple and Triple *Rhyme,* in some other *Poetry* much blamable, are Beauties in this. . . ."[1] This commentator only begins to touch on the art of Butler's couplets; what probably attracted him and his fellow imitators was the apparent carelessness of the form, the license it offered for unbounded "Liberties and Privileges"—always a condition of frequent literary imitation. Nevertheless, the meter of *Hudibras* was closely enough imitated that in 1715 the editors of the *Posthumous Works* of Butler were either fooled themselves or succeeded in fooling the reading public of the day by including in the edition a number of works in Hudibrastics not written by Butler. By 1700, according to Edward Ames Richards's bibliography of Hudibrastic verse, twenty-five works had been published in the meter, and Richmond P. Bond's "Register of Burlesque Poems" lists an additional fifty-six titles before 1750.

Two other features of Hudibrastic imitation—the reuse of Butler's Quixotic fable and the employment of his peculiar satiric method—have been thoroughly canvassed by Richards and Bond and are not discussed here. I can, however, take notice of one other aspect of Hudibrastic influence that these more comprehensive surveys have had to ignore. I have in mind the occurrence in satiric narratives after 1660 of the pattern of Butler's opening lines in *Hudibras*—perhaps the most memorable feature of the poem—that is, the "When . . . When . . . Then . . ." formula or some variation of it. Such a statement implies what cannot, of course, be positively asserted: that Butler invented the pattern. It is surprising that we cannot find so natural an organizing device (*cum . . . tum . . .* in Latin) among the illustrations of traditional schemes in the rhetorical handbooks of the period. Chaucer used a simplified form of it at the beginning of the prologue to the *Canterbury Tales* ("Whan that

Aprille with his shoures soote . . . Whan Zephirus eek with his sweete breeth . . . Thanne longen folk to goon on pilgrimages"); there is a suggestion of it in the opening of the prologue to Langland's *Piers Plowman* ("In a somer seson whan soft was the sonne . . . Thann gan I to meten a merueilouse sweuene"); and it appears frequently and with interesting variations in Shakespeare's sonnets.

In none of these analogues, however, do the words "when" and "then" carry much temporal significance: they function rhetorically, and intransitively, as it were, as a convenient way of expressing the relationship between cause and effect or between motive and action. Butler's use of the words is insistently and transitively temporal, however. "*When* civil fury first grew high" is a metaphor for "in the 1640s" or, as Butler stated on his title page, "in the time of the late Wars"; and "*Then* did Sir Knight abandon dwelling" refers to the same time. The viewpoint is emphatically retrospective, like the "Once upon a time" of a fairytale, or—more probably the case—the "Sithen the siege was ceased" of some romance. In other words, Butler's formulaic opening is an integral part of the rhetoric of burlesque romance; and it may have been so used before it appeared in *Hudibras*. "The Authors Mock-Song to Marke Anthony," published in 1647 and attributed to Butler's good friend John Cleveland, suggests this fact:

> When as the Night-raven sung Pluto's Mattins,
> And *Cerberus* cried three Amens at a hould;
> When night-wandring Witches put on their pattins,
> Midnight as darke as their faces are fould,
> Then did the Furies doome
> That my night-mare should come.[2]

Whatever the source of this temporal pattern, its frequency in burlesque and satire written after the appearance of *Hudibras* strongly suggests its close dependence upon Butler's poem. Very likely, since it was the most easily imitated feature of Butler's style, it recommended itself to the novice. Here, for instance, is the first published work of the later Platonic enthusiast John Norris, a burlesque called "A Murnival of Knaves," which appeared in 1683:

> When that the poor oppressed *Press*
> Groan'd under the *Cacoethes*
> Of Scribling; when *Baboon* and *Pug*

> Skirmisht in Paper-Dialogue;
> When Vile *Tom'sson* did disenbogue
> At one another *Ruffian, Rogue,*
> Profligate *Villain,* Fidler, Knave,
> *Buffon* and *Rascal,* rail and rave
> In such foul terms as these; a Pack
> Enuf to break a *Porters* back,
> Or sham at th' sharpest scolding rate
> The *Wastecoteers* of *Beline's-gate:*
> When one of these loose *Pamphleteers*
> Was very near losing his Ears,
> And did through *Wood-loop-hole* survey
> The Market on a welcome day;
> Nay, had he not begg'd off close-keeping,
> And Fine, good faith, had paid for's peeping:
> Then 'twas.
>
> (ll. 1–19)

Clearly, Norris was not a Butler: he was uncomfortably cramped in Hudibrastics (the roomy Pindaric was to become his favorite mode of expression), and his wit is hackneyed ("oppressed *Press*") and humorless (though later he does manage to rhyme *"Sister"* with "kist her"). More in the spirit of *Hudibras* are four eighteenth-century burlesques by Butler's best-known imitator, Ned Ward (1667–1731): *Hudibras Redivivius* (1705), *England's Reformation From the time of King Henry The VIIIth To the End of Oate's Plot* (1710), *Vulgus Britannicus* (1710), and *British Wonders* (1717). All exemplify the hudibrastic opening, but *England's Reformation* comes closest perhaps to the satiric texture of Ward's model:

> When Old King *Harry* Youthful grew,
> As Eagles do, or Hawks in Mew,
> And did in spite of *Pope* and *Fate,*
> Behead, Ripp, and Repudiate
> Those too-too long liv'd things his Wives.
> With Axes, Bills, and Midwives Knives:
> When he the Papal Power rejected,
> And from the Church the Realm Dissected
> And in the great St. *PETERS* stead
> Proclaim'd himself the Churches Head.
> When he his Ancient *Queen* forsook,
> And Buxom *Anna Bollen* took,

> Then in the *Noddle* of the Nation
> He bred the Maggot *Reformation*.[3]

Ward's three other specimens illustrate a recurring modification of Butler's burlesque pattern, the blending with it of elements of the more authentically heroic opening of Dryden's *Absalom and Achitophel* ("In pious times, e'r Priest-craft did begin"). Ward's *Vulgus Britannicus*, for instance, begins

> In Spiteful Times when *Humane Folly*,
> Discourag'd all that's Good and Holy;
> When *Peace* and *Truth* were out of Season,
> And *Zeal* had got the start of *Reason*[4]

and in 1723, an anonymous satire entitled *The Pettifoggers* (a subject Butler would certainly have approved) brought *Absalom and Achitophel* and *Hudibras* even more closely together by setting Butler's time-specific "When" in a mythical golden age of freedom:

> In ancient Days, when Times were good,
> And Men lov'd Peace and Neighborhood;
> When all with one another bore,
> None were deem'd either Rogue or Whore;
> .  .  .  .  .  .  .  .  .  .  .  .
> Then was Old *England* free, at least,
> From Lawyers as from Rav'nous Beast.[5]

Dryden's more varied and less specific sequence of temporal states soon became the standard feature of the hudibrastic opening. Thus in 1698 an octosyllabic satire entitled *The Progress* (attributed to Henry Mildmay) sustained a series of temporal adverbs and prepositions (including "In former days . . . When honesty no crime was thought . . . Ere tailor's yards were scepters made; / Before each coffee club durst prate . . .") for fifty-nine lines before at last concluding "I say, ere all these things befell, / Which now long since, no tongue can tell; / Then were the Golden Days, if any."[6] Clearly, *The Progress* establishes some sort of record in the use of the device.

What I have called the "retrospective" note of the opening of *Hudibras* is missing in many of these imitations of the poem, and its absence accounts for much of the difference between them and their model. Edward Ames Richards makes a related point when he describes one of the moods of *Hudibras* as "a satiric song of victory." "One might infer," he says, "that Dissent and Presbyterianism had been wiped out in 1660."[7] That is not to say that Butler shared Dryden's view of the Restoration as "A Series of new time," a redemption of time. Time merely revolved for Butler. He could be neither nostalgic about the past nor optimistic about the future, and in *Hudibras* he reviewed the bad-old-days of the Commonwealth from the bad-new-days of the Restoration. But from the vantage point of the present in which he wrote the poem, at least one revolution was complete; the immediate past had taken shape, and this freed him from the seriousness of narrow party satire, allowing him to broaden his satiric perspective and indulge his inventiveness. In short, victory made ridiculing the Puritans fun. Most hudibrastic imitations, however, were written in the heat of party strife. They tend, therefore, to be defensive, narrowly doctrinaire, and too preoccupied with the pressing affairs of the moment to permit the witty invention that everywhere pervades Butler's poem. Hastily thrown together, they manage at best to convey only the raciness of their original—and that, as it were, is by necessity rather than choice. Norris's *Murnival of Knaves,* the first of the imitative openings cited in this chapter, was published in June 1683 as a reaction to the abortive Whig attack that same month upon Charles II, the so-called Rye House Plot. For Norris, therefore, "When . . . When . . . Then" refers to the present; the sole function of the device was to announce the fact that its author was on the right side—on Butler's side. Indeed, as Edward Ames Richards suggests, the periodic emergence of Hudibrastic imitation serves as an index to the rise of Puritanism, Dissent, Catholicism—and, for that matter, any threat to the existing establishment.

Thus in England, Thomas D'Urfey (1653–1723), best known for a compilation of songs entitled *Pills to Purge Melancholy,* published in the year Butler died a continuation of the adventures of Hudibras and Ralpho called *Butler's Ghost,* a work of Tory propaganda that plays upon the parallel between political affairs in 1680 and in the 1640s.[8] Just before he died, Butler himself, it will be recalled, planned to release an old, hitherto unpublished prose tract, *The Case of King Charles I Truly Stated,* for this purpose, and a year later, Dryden responded to the same threat with *Absalom and Achitophel.* Hudibrastics were again pressed into service at the time of the English Settlement, in D'Urfey's *Collin's Walk* (1690); during the Jacobite threat, in the anonymous *Pendragon, or the Carpet Knight;* at the time of the settlement of the national church in Scotland, in *A Mock Poem, upon the Expedition of the Highland-host . . . 1678* by

William Cleland; and at the rise of Methodism, in the anonymous attack upon the preacher George Whitefield entitled *The Methodists*.

Of course, not all political satire in the eighteenth century was Hudibrastic; in Britain, the idiom competed with the more disciplined heroic couplet. In America, however, this competition was less marked. We might well imagine that Americans found the satiric voices of Dryden and Pope rather aristocratic for their tastes; Butler's, on the other hand, must have seemed like one of the proletariat. Notwithstanding its author's loyalist and conservative attitudes, *Hudibras* laughingly reassured the American patriots that the aristocratic traditions they had cast off were indeed absurd, and to such a voice they would have listened with complete understanding. For this reason, as Elizabeth Cook indicates, "the native American satiric verse more often followed Butler's *Hudibras*" than the works of their more immediate contemporaries.[9] Bruce Granger counts "no fewer than seventy-seven Hudibrastic poems treating of matters political . . . in America,"[10] and to these could be added scores of minor works—songs, ballads, elegies, and the like—that reveal Butler's influence one way or another.

At least a part of the currency of Hudibrastics in America may be attributed to the proprietary care given the form by John Trumbull, Butler's most eminent American imitator, whose *M'Fingal*, completed in 1782, popularized the style. Of all the imitations mentioned thus far, *M'Fingal* is perhaps the only one that can be called an artistic achievement in its own right, and it may be significant that Trumbull is one of the few imitators of *Hudibras* who did not begin by attempting to duplicate his model. His own artistic integrity and his respect for *Hudibras* as an inimitable original did not permit the sort of slavish imitation we have been considering. "The Critical Reader," he wrote, "will discern that I have rather proposed to myself Swift and Churchill as models in my Hudibrastic writings, than the Author of Hudibras. I have sometimes had Butler's manner in my eye, for a few lines, but was soon forced to quit it. Indeed his kind of wit & the oddity of his Comparisons was in my Opinion never well imitated by any man, nor ever will be."[11] This statement does not say that the presence of *Hudibras* is not to be felt in the poem; a glance at the opening lines of the first canto of *M'Fingal* dispells that notion:

> WHEN YANKIES, skill'd in martial rule,
>     First put the British troops to school;
>     Instructed them in warlike trade,

And new manoeuvres of parade;
The true war-dance of Yanky-reels,
And manual exercise of heels;
Made them give up, like saints complete,
The arm of flesh and trust the feet,
And work, like Christians undissembling,
Salvation out, by fear and trembling;
.  .  .  .  .  .  .  .  .  .  .  .
From Boston, in his best array,
Great 'Squire M'Fingal took his way. [12]

Here again is the familiar "when" clause, out of which the peripatetic hero makes his way. But the temporal pattern is only implicit, and there is little attempt to reproduce Butler's rhyme effects. M'Fingal's burlesque credentials are solid: he is a Scot and a clairvoyant (Trumbull took the name from the Ossianic pseudoepic *Fingal* by James Macpherson). But the hero does not remain true to his original principles; he becomes a high-churchman and a loyal king's man who turns his clairvoyance to loyalist prophecies that his patriotic countrymen force him to retract. The differences between *Hudibras* and *M'Fingal* may be explained by the great social and political revolutions that had occurred in the century separating Butler from Trumbull, and it is interesting to watch the American adapt the older satiric vehicle to new purposes. At the same time, we must give at least qualified assent to Edward Ames Richards's statement that "*M'Fingal* is a perfect justification of the fears and scorn expressed by Butler. . . . For it exhibits Dissent in its own self-contained society, with its own conventions, with the desire and the power to look askance at other forms of religious and political propriety. The wheel turns slowly, but it turns." [13]

Society expects us to undervalue imitations and to honor originals. I conclude this study in the hope that I have performed this obligation for Butler. I must, however, since my original is *Hudibras,* guard against complacency in this act; for if there is one overriding concern in Butler's work, it is the exposure of self-delusion, of saying what we do not really believe. That *Hudibras,* then, should be the subject of such petty dishonesty, that I should attempt here to make extravagant claims about its place in our literature, would be richly ironic. Butler could have turned such an effort to satiric capital in a Character of "A Modern Critic of *Hudibras*": "He is one who has learned that opinion in

unfamiliar matters passes most easily . . . ," it might begin. Samuel
Pepys, after two attempts to appreciate Butler's poem, confessed in his
diary that he simply did not "see enough where the wit lies." If Pepys
had the courage to say as much in public, his opinion deserves our
respect, for, before anything else, *Hudibras* demands an honest response
from its readers.

In our own time, Butler's poem has received such a response from
Earl Miner. In a chapter of his *Restoration Mode* (1974) entitled "Hating
Our Physician" (the satirist is our physician, and as Butler noted in his
prose observations, "People can never endure those, that seeke to re-
cover them from their deare Dotage" [22:4]), Miner describes *Hudibras*
as "the worst great poem in the language," and Butler as "indisputably
one of the worst as well as one of the great poets in the language."[14]
Here is the honesty that Butler demands in our criticism of *Hudibras*.
Miner refuses to ignore (as we all must) the "messiness" of the poem and
the ignominy of its ideas, its sheer quantity of ugliness. But then if we
read Butler patiently and attentively, he does not let us ignore the
ugliness: he forces us even to consent to the integrity of his own vision
of it. I must agree with Professor Miner that there is not only something terrible in this sort of greatness,[15] but something great in this
sort of ugliness.

I must, then, also assume that Butler was aware of the ugliness of
*Hudibras*. The poem presents itself as a calculated reaction to the idea of
"great" literature, to a tradition of "classic" norms, of literature as the
paradigm of humanness, the vehicle of a viable past. A poem in a
tradition presents itself in a line of succession from works that precede
it, and it begins with an assurance of the usefulness of those works to
itself. Tradition creates a space in which a new work can locate itself. It
furnishes a system of meaning, a model of artistic expectations, and it
imposes upon the poet a "voice" through which he utters not whatever
he pleases, nor even everything his integrity dictates, but only what is
pertinent to a grand enterprise. In effect, tradition *re-places* the poet.

My earlier discussion of Butler's literary criticism—in particular, his
repudiation of established norms as disguises of human weaknesses—
makes it clear that he would have had little reason to think of himself as
a poet writing in a literary tradition. Of course, *Hudibras* makes ironic
reference to earlier literature; but this is the detritus of that tradition
which makes up much of the "mess" of the poem. But its primary
reference, as I noticed in its retrospective opening lines and in its play
with the elements of carnival and popular festivity, is to the real world.

*Hudibras,* then, declines a place in the tradition, *dis-places* itself there, and in doing so forces the reader to repudiate the tradition because the works that comprise it do not represent life as it is, and because the tradition cannot make room for a work that uncompromisingly does represent it as it is. But in situating itself outside the literary tradition, *Hudibras* may have established another tradition. In 1976 David Vieth argued that along-side the " 'official' literary lineage of Denham-Waller-Milton-Dryden-Pope," there is "a competing, equally important line" beginning with Butler and including such writers as Bucking-ham, Rochester, Swift, the later Pope, and Sterne. The distinctive features of Vieth's "unofficial" tradition (which is modeled upon twentieth-century absurdist lines) include immediacy of experience and an awareness of its inherent ironies, an unstable point of view that raises questions about the identity of speakers, and formal open-endedness,[16] qualities we have recognized in the Menippean and carnivalesque features of *Hudibras.* Margaret Anne Doody also attaches enduring importance to the real world materials of *Hudibras.* The Augustans, she writes, did not read the poetry of their time "for static mimesis of a quiet universe of quiet things," but for images of "people, animals, things mixed up and rioting." The traditional genres had to go, therefore, "because they don't assume enough of reality." Doody goes on to quote Butler's description of the skimmington, not merely as an illustration of this view, but as an instance of what, she argues, would become "a common *topos* of Augustan poetry."[17] It may be a mistake to associate Butler too closely with the Augustans (and more of a mistake to imagine him sublimating his discontent in populist ideology); but Vieth and Doody are both responding, I think, to an important quality of *Hudibras.* In rejecting the unitary voice imposed by the tradition, Butler opened his poem to the polyphony of discourses of his time and in so doing made his own integrity the medium of *Hudibras.* One wonders whether this may not be the reason that in his lifetime the title of his poem was attached to his name, so that he became Hudibras Butler.

As we have seen from many of his Characters and prose observations, Butler regarded ancient tradition and modern learning alike as avenues of escape from the unpleasant facts of human experience; so it is unlikely that he paid much attention to the famous controversy of his time between the defenders of ancient and modern learning. From our vantage point, however, Butler appears as the first important literary "Modern," using this word now as a descriptive rather than an evaluative term. Even with this qualification, however, we are likely to be unhappy with the characterization of Butler as Modern. The label appears to ignore the fact that his foremost admirers in the next generation were the Modern-baiting Scriblerians, men such as Swift and Pope and John Garth; and, of course, it condemns him by association with their enemies, Thomas Hobbes, William Wotton, Richard Bentley, and their like—not to mention Swift's Grub-Street narrator of *A Tale of a Tub* and the morose and dirty spider of his *Battle of the Books*. We may now see that it was to Butler's credit that his most distinguished apostles have come from hostile quarters and that his greatest value is still to teach us that all human distinctions are at bottom self-serving and not to be trusted. The perfect integrity of Butler's vision of human weakness and the totality of his contempt for it separates only himself from all the others.

# Notes and References

*Chapter One*

1. Samuel Johnson, *Lives of the English Poets,* ed. G. B. Hill (Oxford: Clarendon Press, 1905), 1:209.

2. An annotation in William Oldys's 1726 edition of *Hudibras* attributes this "Life" to Sir J. Anstrey [James Astry]. See "Oldys' Notes on *Hudibras,*" *Notes and Queries,* 3rd ser. 3 (1863):101–2.

3. See John Wilders's introduction to *Hudibras* (Oxford: Clarendon Press, 1967), xiii, and E. S. de Beer, "The Later Life of Samuel Butler," *Review of English Studies* 4 (1928):159–60. Johnson apparently also had access to the notes of T. R. Nash, whose biography of the poet appeared in an edition of *Hudibras* published in 1793.

4. Johnson, *Lives,* 201.

5. Important bits of biographical information have been uncovered, however, by René Lamar, Ricardo Quintana, Norma Bentley, and Michael Wilding.

6. The most detailed account of Butler's childhood is René Lamar's "Du nouveau sur l'auteur d'*Hudibras:* Samuel Butler en Worcestershire," *Revue Anglo-Américaine* 1 (1924):213–27. See also R. M. Wilding, "The Date of Samuel Butler's Baptism," *Review of English Studies* 17 (1966): 174–77.

7. See Michael Wilding, "Samuel Butler at Barbourne," *Notes and Queries* n. s. 13 (1966):17.

8. Wilders, introduction to *Hudibras,* xvii.

9. See René Lamar, "Samuel Butler à l'École du Roi," *Études anglaises* 5 (1952):17–24.

10. Wilding, "Samuel Butler at Barbourne," 17–18.

11. Wilders, introduction to *Hudibras,* xvii.

12. The phrase comes from Butler's Character "An Antiquary" in *Samuel Butler 1612–1680: Characters,* edited by Charles W. Daves (Cleveland: Press of Case Western Reserve University, 1970), 77. Subsequent quotations from the Characters are from this edition.

13. Butler identifies only one passage from Selden in his notebook, however. See *Prose Observations,* ed. Hugh de Quehen (Oxford: Clarendon Press, 1979), 40; see also de Quehen's commentary, 400. Throughout this study, I cite this edition of Butler's prose notebook material.

14. John Aubrey, *Brief Lives,* ed. Andrew Clark (Oxford: Clarendon Press, 1898), 1:135.

15. Hardin Craig, "*Hudibras,* Part I, and the Politics of 1647," in *The Manly Anniversary Studies in Language and Literature* (Chicago: University of Chicago Press, 1923), 147.

16. Wilders, *Hudibras,* 452. Wilders reviews the evidence for and against accepting Luke as the model of Hudibras in Appendix B of his edition of the poem, the text I use throughout this study. Quotations are normally identified parenthetically by part, canto, and line.

17. Ricardo Quintana, "The Butler-Oxenden Correspondence," *Modern Language Notes* 48 (1933):3. Wilders quotes both letters in Appendix A of his edition of *Hudibras.*

18. Ibid., 4.

19. Ibid., 7. Wilders (xlvi) points out literary allusions in part 1 of the poem to works that were published even after the Restoration.

20. Aubrey, *Brief Lives,* 1:174–75.

21. Ibid., 1:136; Wilders, introduction to *Hudibras,* xviii. See also Michael Wilding, "Butler and Gray's Inn," *Notes and Queries,* n. s., 18 (1971):293–95: "It seems likely that Butler . . . had some legal connections."

22. *Characters,* 113, 102, 114. See also De Quehen's index listing for "law and lawyers" in *Prose Observations,* and René Lamar, "Samuel Butler et la Justice de son Temps," *Études anglaises,* 7 (1954):271–79.

23. Quintana, "Butler-Oxenden," 4.

24. René Lamar, *Satires and Miscellaneous Poetry and Prose* (Cambridge: Cambridge University Press, 1928), 266. John Cook is burned in effigy in the Rump-burning episode of *Hudibras* (3:2, l. 1650). Lamar's *Satires* reprints all the works attributed to Butler mentioned in this paragraph, with the exception of Lord Roos's *Answer*; it is my source for Butler's minor verse, hereafter referred to parenthetically as *Satires.*

25. A. H. De Quehen, "An Account of Works Attributed to Samuel Butler," *Review of English Studies,* 33 (1982):275. Prynne is mentioned by name in the mock-invocation to *Hudibras* (1:1, l. 640) and elsewhere in the poem and in the Characters (see especially the Character of "An Haranguer," 98).

26. De Quehen, "An Account," 275. Details of the scandal are given by J. Milton French in *The Life Records of John Milton* (New Brunswick: Rutger's University Press, 1958), 5, 11–15. See also C. J. Hindle, "A Broadside by Samuel Butler," *Times Literary Supplement* (21 March 1936), 244.

27. Paul Bunyan Anderson argues assiduously, but unconvincingly, I now believe, to attribute to Butler three more controversial prose works, *The Character of the Rump, The Censure of the Rota Upon Mr. Milton's Book* . . . (both published in 1660), and *The Transproser Rehears'd* (1673). See "Anonymous Critic of Milton: Richard Leigh? or Butler?" *Studies in Philology,* 44 (1947):504–18.

28. Quintana, "Butler-Oxenden," 4.

29. See Peter Cunningham, "The Author of *Hudibras* at Ludlow Castle," *Notes and Queries,* 1st ser., 5 (1852):5–6.

30. Wilders, introduction to *Hudibras,* xix.

31. Pepys's diary entry is dated 6 February 1663.

32. Wilders, introduction to *Hudibras,* liv–lv.

33. Ibid., xlvii.

34. James L. Thorson, "The Publication of *Hudibras,*" *Papers of the Bibliographical Society of America,* 60 (1966):423, 432–34.

35. Aubrey, *Brief Lives,* 1: 136.

36. De Beer, "The Later Life," 164; Aubrey, *Brief Lives,* 1: 136.

37. Anthony à Wood, *Athenae Oxinienses,* ed. Philip Bliss (London: 1813–20), 3: 875.

38. The letter is printed in Lamar's edition of the *Satires,* p. 399; see also Aubrey, *Brief Lives,* 1: 136.

39. Thyer's prefatory remarks on the Characters (first printed in the *Genuine Remains*) are reprinted in Waller's edition of *Characters and Passages from Note-Books* (Cambridge: Cambridge University Press, 1908), 481.

40. De Quehan, *Prose Observations,* xxvi; see also his essay "Editing Butler's Manuscripts," in *Editing Seventeenth-Century Prose,* ed. D. I. B. Smith (Toronto: Hakkert, 1972), 81.

41. De Quehen, "Editing Butler's Manuscripts," 81; *Prose Observations,* xxvi.

42. John Harold Wilson, *The Court Wits of the Restoration: An Introduction* (New York: Octagon Books, 1967), 178.

43. See Norma E. Bentley, "Hudibras Butler Abroad," *Modern Language Notes,* 40 (1945):254–59.

44. Harold Brooks, "The 'Imitation' in English Poetry, Especially in Formal Satire, Before the Age of Pope," *Review of English Studies* 25 (1949):127–32.

45. *History of the Royal Society,* ed. Jackson I. Cope and Harold Whitmore Jones (St. Louis: Washington University Press, 1958), 417.

46. Marjorie Nicolson's early dating of at least a preliminary draft of the octosyllabic version of "The Elephant" deserves consideration, I believe; see *Pepys' "Diary" and the New Science* (Charlottesville: University Press of Virginia, 1965), 152, 157. 1675–76 is more generally accepted as the date of the final draft of this version, followed shortly by the pentameter version.

47. DeBeer, "The Later Life," 163. The visit to The Hague is suggested by several prose observations (184, 301) and by a short poetic description of Holland (*Satires,* 149).

48. Nicolson, *Pepys' "Diary" and the New Science,* 151–52. For recent attempts to date the two versions of "The Elephant in the Moon," see Sv.

Brunn, "The Date of Samuel Butler's *The Elephant in the Moon*," *English Studies* 55 (1974):133–39, and Guy Laprevotte, "*The Elephant in the Moon* de Samuel Butler: le Contexte et la Satire," *Etudes anglaises* 15 (1972):465–78.

49. The injunction is reprinted in Jan Veldkamp's *Samuel Butler: The Author of Hudibras* (Hilversum: De Atlas, 1923), 22–23. A similar injunction had been issued to Butler in 1663, according to DeBeer, "The Later Life," (162).

50. Wilders, introduction to *Hudibras*, lvi.

51. Ibid., xx.

52. H. F. Brooks, "Gift to Samuel Butler," *Times Literary Supplement*, (6 July 1940) 327.

53. "The Parish of St. Paul Covent Garden," in *Survey of London*, vol. 37 ed. F. H. W. Sheppard (London: 1970), 183.

54. The "Preface to the Reader" in the 1691 edition remarks that "it was Mr. *Butler's* design to Print the Discourse himself, had not Death prevented Him" (*Satires*, 367, italics reversed). The occasion for this later printing was still another avatar "of the old Republican Stamp," Edmund Ludlow's *Letter* to Sir Edward Seymour "comparing the Tyranny of the first four years of King Charles the Martyr with the Tyranny of the four year's Reign of the late abdicated King."

55. De Quehen, "Editing Butler's Manuscripts," 71.

56. Ibid., 72, 82.

57. Johnson, *Lives*, 1: 122.

58. De Quehen, "Editing Butler's Manuscripts," 74.

59. Ibid., 91–92.

60. Josephine Bauer, "Some Verse Fragments and Prose *Characters* by Samuel Butler Not Included in the *Complete Works*," *Modern Philology*, 45 (1948):162.

*Chapter Two*

1. Unless otherwise indicated, figures in parentheses refer to page and paragraph in De Quehen's *Prose Observations*.

2. Ricardo Quintana, "Samuel Butler: A Restoration Figure in a Modern Light," *English Literary History* 18 (1951):14–15. General discussions of Butler's thought may also be found in Dan Gibson, Jr., "Samuel Butler," in *Seventeenth Century Studies*, ed. Robert Shafer (Princeton: Princeton University Press, 1933), 277–335; Norma Bentley's Ph.D. dissertation, "Hudibras Butler" (Syracuse University, 1944); John Wilders's introduction to *Hudibras*, xxi–xxviii; George Wasserman, "Samuel Butler and the Problem of Unnatural Man," *Modern Language Quarterly* 31 (1970):179–94; De Quehen's introduction to the *Prose Observations*, xxv–xxxviii; and Kevin L. Cope, "The Infinite

Perimeter: Human Nature and Ethical Mediation in Six Restoration Writers," *Restoration* 5 (1981):58–75.

3. Jackson I. Cope, *Joseph Glanvill: Anglican Apologist* (St. Louis: Washington University Press, 1956), 110.

4. Don Cameron Allen, *The Legend of Noah: Renaissance Rationalism in Art, Science, and Letters* (Urbana, University of Illinois Press, 1963), 23.

5. Paul Fussell, *The Rhetorical World of Augustan Humanism* (Oxford: Oxford University Press, 1965), 232.

6. Ibid., 222.

7. William C. Horne, "Curiosity and Ridicule in Samuel Butler's Satire on Science," *Restoration* 7 (1983):10; Ken Robinson, "The Skepticism of Butler's Satire on Science: Optimistic or Pessimistic," in the same issue of *Restoration,* p. 4.

8. Nicolson (*Pepys' "Diary" and the New Science*) has identified several of the speakers in the satire as members of the Royal Society. See also Sv. Brunn, "Who's Who in Samuel Butler's *The Elephant in the Moon,*" *English Studies,* 50 (1969):381–89.

9. Thomas Hobbes, "The Answer to D'Avenant," in *Critical Essays of the Seventeenth Century,* ed. J. E. Spingarn (Oxford: Clarendon Press, 1908), 2, 56.

10. Kevin L. Cope, "The Conquest of Truth: Wycherley, Rochester, Butler, and Dryden and the Restoration Critique of Satire," *Restoration* 10 (1986):22.

11. Michael A. Seidel, "Patterns of Anarchy and Oppression in Samuel Butler's *Hudibras,*" *Eighteenth-Century Studies* 5 (1971–72):296–97.

12. Ibid., 298.

13. Quintana, "Samuel Butler," 28.

14. Ruth Nevo, *The Dial of Virtue* (Princeton: Princeton University Press, 1963), 235.

15. Seidel, "Patterns of Anarchy," 299–300.

16. Michael Seidel, "The Internecine Romance: Butler's *Hudibras,*" in *Satiric Inheritance: Rabelais to Sterne* (Princeton: Princeton University Press, 1979), 130.

17. A. D. Cousins, "The Idea of a 'Restoration' and the Verse Satires of Butler and Marvell," *Southern Review* 14 (1981):131–42.

18. Fussell, *Augustan Humanism,* 172.

19. Seventeenth-century Anglican rationalism is clearly defined by Philip Harth in *Swift and Anglican Rationalism* (Chicago: University of Chicago Press, 1961).

20. Bentley, "Hudibras Butler," 120; De Quehen, *Prose Observations,* lix–lx.

21. My source for this passage is Bentley's dissertation, "Hudibras But-

ler," 120. It is possible, since I have not been able to locate the passage in the *Prose Observations,* that De Quehen identified it as one of Longueville's own commonplace entires. Even so, the thought is quite consistent with Butler's observations elsewhere. See *Prose Observations,* 81, 149:1.

*Chapter Three*

1. Ricardo Quintana, "The Butler-Oxenden Correspondence," *Modern Language Notes* 48 (1933):4.
2. See Ian Jack, *Augustan Satire: Intention and Idiom in English Poetry: 1660–1750* (Oxford: Clarendon Press, 1952), 15–16. See also G. W. Duffett, "The Name 'Hudibras,' " *Notes and Queries* 9 (1935):96.
3. Wilders's commentary to *Hudibras,* 330, 343.
4. Butler's letter to Oxenden, in Quintana, "Butler-Oxenden," 4.
5. See Wilder's introduction to *Hudibras,* xxxiii, and Michael Wilding, "Flecknoe's 'Diarium': A Source for 'Hudibras,' " *Notes and Queries* 22 (1975):310–12.
6. William C. Horne, "Butler's Use of the *Rump* in *Hudibras,*" *Library Chronicle,* 37 (1971):126–35.
7. Jan Veldkamp studies Butler's relation to Cervantes and Rabelais in the last two chapters of his *Samuel Butler: The Author of Hudibras.* See also Albert H. West, *L'influence française dans la poésie burlesque en Angleterre entre 1660 et 1700* (New York: Burt Franklin, 1971), 105–55.
8. Michael Seidel, *Satiric Inheritance,* 129.
9. Ibid., 130–31.
10. See especially Bakhtin's *Rabelais and His World,* trans. Helene Iswolsky (Bloomington: Indiana University Press, 1984).
11. Seidel, *Satiric Inheritance,* 125.
12. See the analysis of Ralpho by W. O. S. Sutherland, Jr., in his *The Art of the Satirist* (Austin: University of Texas Press, 1965), pp. 65–66.
13. Quoted from Ellen Douglass Leyburn's *"Hudibras* Considered as a Satiric Allegory," *Huntington Library Quarterly* 16 (1953):155.
14. See J. Donovan, "The 'Key to Hudibras' and Cleveland's 'The Character of a London Diurnall,' " *Notes and Queries,* 20 (1973):175–76. Wilders includes the most important identifications from the "Key" in his commentary; see *Hudibras,* 330, 341.
15. Craig, *"Hudibras,* Part I, and the Politics of 1647," 151–53.
16. W. S. Miller, "The Allegory in Part I of *Hudibras,*" *Huntington Library Quarterly,* 21 (1958), 326.
17. Ibid. At the end of her doctoral dissertation, Norma Bentley sketches a psychological interpretation of *Hudibras* that arrives at a point not too far from Miller's conclusion. See "Hudibras Butler," 202–12.
18. Wilders, introduction to *Hudibras,* xliv–xlvi.

19. Miller, "The Allegory in Part I of *Hudibras*," 324.

20. Ibid., 328.

21. Earl Miner, *The Restoration Mode from Milton to Dryden* (Princeton: Princeton University Press, 1974), 189, 477.

22. Paul J. Korshin, *Typologies in England: 1650–1820* (Princeton: Princeton University Press, 1982), 277–82.

23. Alvin Kernan, *The Plot of Satire* (New Haven: Yale University Press, 1965), 4.

24. Ibid., 3.

25. Ibid., 4.

26. William Horne's analysis of the category of "hard words" includes also contentious and cacophonous language. See his "Hard Words in *Hudibras*," *Durham University Journal* 75 (1983):31–43.

27. Linda Troost, "Poetry, Politics, and Puddings: The Imagery of Food in Butler's *Hudibras*," *Restoration* 9 (1985):85.

28. Richmond P. Bond, *English Burlesque Poetry: 1700–1750* (Cambridge: Harvard University Press, 1932), 5.

29. Ibid., 4.

30. Ibid., 6.

31. James Sutherland, *English Literature of the Late Seventeenth Century* (Oxford: Oxford University Press, 1969), 160.

32. Wilders, introduction to *Hudibras*, xxxv.

33. Edward Ames Richards, *Hudibras in the Burlesque Tradition* (New York: Columbia University Press, 1937), x, 121.

34. Nevo, *Dial of Virtue*, 192.

35. Jack, *Augustan Satire*, 23–24, 46.

36. David Farley-Hills, *Rochester's Poetry* (London: Bell and Hyman, 1978), 92, 103–104.

37. Ibid., 104.

38. Quoted by Karl Shapiro and Robert Benn in *A Prosody Handbook* (New York: Harper and Row, 1965), 188.

39. Nevo, *Dial of Virtue*, 192.

40. The Spectator, no. 59 (8 May 1711) and no. 60 (9 May 1711).

41. Alexander Pope, *Peri Bathous*, in *The Art of Sinking in Poetry*, ed. Edna Leake Steeves (New York, 1952), chap. 12.

42. Kernan, *Plot of Satire*, 171.

43. Mikhail Bakhtin, *Problems of Dostoevsky's Poetics*, ed. and trans. Caryl Emerson (Minneapolis: University of Minnesota Press, 1984), 113.

44. Ibid., 114.

45. See, for example, Edward Dowden, *Puritan and Anglican: Studies in Literature* (New York: Henry Holt, 1901), 279–310; Veldkamp, *Samuel Butler*, 90–93. Albert West, however, discounts these similarities to the menippea; see *L'influence française dans la poésie burlesque en Angleterre entre 1660*

*et 1700* (New York: Burt Franklin, 1971), pp. 105–55. Nash said "Mr. Butler had certainly read it [the menippea] with attention, yet he cannot be said to imitate it." Quoted by Veldkamp, *Samuel Butler,* 93.

46. The phrase is Craig Howes's, in "Rhetorics of Attack: Bakhtin and the Aesthetics of Satire," *Genre* 18 (1986):234.

47. Ibid., 235.

48. W. O. S. Sutherland argues for such a change in *The Art of the Satirist,* pp. 67–68.

49. Susan Staves, *Players' Scepters: Fictions of Authority in the Restoration* (Lincoln: University of Nebraska Press, 1979), 214.

50. See Nicolas H. Nelson, "Astrology, *Hudibras,* and the Puritans," *Journal of the History of Ideas* 37 (1976):521–36.

51. *The Diary of Thomas Burton, Esq.,* quoted by Bentley in "Hudibras Butler," 192.

52. W. O. S. Sutherland, *Art of the Satirist,* 71.

53. Miner, *Restoration Mode,* 170, 475–79.

*Chapter Four*

1. The satire on man is discussed by Bertrand A. Goldgar in "Satires on Man and 'The Dignity of Human Nature,' " *Publications of the Modern Language Association* 80 (1965):535–41; see also W. B. Carnochan, *Lemuel Gulliver's Mirror for Man* (Berkeley: University of California Press, 1968).

2. George Boas, *The Happy Beast in French Thought of the Seventeenth Century* (Baltimore: Johns Hopkins University Press, 1933); see also James E. Gill, "Beast over Man: Theriophilic Paradox in Gulliver's 'Voyage to the Country of the Houyhnhnms,' " *Studies in Philology* 67 (1970):532–49.

3. Horne, "Curiosity and Ridicule in Samuel Butler's Satire on Science," 14.

4. The literary use of the concept of animals as machines is treated by Wallace Shugg in "The Cartesian Beast-Machine in English Literature (1663–1750)," *Journal of the History of Ideas* 29 (1968):279–92. Butler receives little more than passing mention in this study. See also Leonora Cohen Rosenfield, *From Beast-Machine to Man-Machine: Animal Soul in French Letters from Descartes to La Mettrie* (New York: Columbia University Press, 1941).

5. Boas, *Happy Beast,* 1–2.

6. Wilders, commentary, *Hudibras,* 323.

7. Horne, "Hard Words in *Hudibras,*" 31, 34–36.

8. See Butler's note to 1:1, ll. 529–30.

9. See Butler's note to 1:3, l. 134.

10. Lawrence Stone, *The Family, Sex and Marriage in England 1500–1800* (New York: Harper & Row, 1972), 340.

11. The words are Daniel Toutville's, quoted by C. A. Patrides, in

*Milton and the Christian Tradition* (Oxford: Oxford University Press, 1966), p. 67.

12. Felicity A. Nussbaum, *The Brink of All We Hate: English Satires on Women 1660–1750* (Lexington: University of Kentucky Press, 1984), 56.

13. Miner, *Restoration Mode,* 188.

14. William C. Horne, " 'Between th' Petticoat and Breeches': Sexual Warfare and the Marriage Debate in *Hudibras*" in *Studies in Eighteenth-Century Culture,* ed. Harry C. Payne, vol. 11 (Madison: University of Wisconsin Press, 1982), 138–39.

15. Compare Marvell's definition of a skimmington in "Last Instructions to a Painter": "A Punishment invented first to awe / Masculine Wives, transgressing Natural Law." Quoted by Wilders, commentary, *Hudibras,* 386.

16. John Milton, *Works,* ed. Frank A. Patterson, vol. 3 (New York: Columbia University Press, 1931–40), 475.

17. Quoted by John Halkell in *Milton and the Idea of Matrimony* (New Haven: Yale University Press, 1970), 52.

18. Nevo, *Dial of Virtue,* 230.

19. Philip Harth, "Studies in Restoration Literature," *Philological Quarterly,* 56 (1977):435.

20. *Satires,* 220.

21. Ibid., 211.

22. Mikhail Bakhtin, *Problems of Dostoevsky's Poetics,* trans. Caryl Emerson (Minneapolis: University of Minnesota Press, 1984), 130–31. My chief debt to Bakhtin is to the discussion of carnival in his *Rabelais and His World,* trans. Helene Iswolsky (Bloomington: Indiana University Press, 1984), passim. Subsequent references in this chapter to the latter book will be made parenthetically.

23. Terry Castle, *Masquerade and Civilization* (Stanford: Stanford University Press, 1986), 75–76.

24. Paul Korshin is no doubt right that Ralpho's argument parodies typological exegesis and effectively satirizes "the more obscurantist branches of mysticism." But to turn the satire entirely upon Ralpho at this point in the poem is to ignore both the comic climax of part 1 and the conclusion of Ralpho's argument, where, without the use of typology, he asserts that "ev'ry Synod [is] but a Fair" (1:3, l. 1148). See Korshin, *Typologies in England,* 277–78.

25. The phrase is taken from Nussbaum's *The Brink of All We Hate,* p. 54.

26. For instance, William Francis Smith, in the chapter on Butler in *The Cambridge History of English Literature,* vol. 8 (New York: G. P. Putnam, 1912), pp. 65–90, traces the roots of the poem to medieval satires on women and the mendicant orders; Jan Veldkamp observed: "on the question of women Butler is . . . at one with Rabelais," *Samuel Butler,* p. 226.

27. External evidence of the presence of this carnival pattern in Butler's poem is suggested by the spurious *Hudibras: the Second Part* (1663), the un-

known author of which anticipated the whipping of the authentic knight by
having the counterfeit Hudibras—as Sidrophel reports in Butler's *Second
Part*—"bang'd, both back and side wel" (2: 3, 1. 994) for attempting to
interfere with some May games at Kingston.

28. Martin Ingram, "Ridings, Rough Music and Popular Culture," *Past
and Present* 105 (1984):86.

29. The interesting implications of this fact are taken up in Jean-
Christophe Agnew's *Worlds Apart: The Market and the Theater in Anglo-
American Thought, 1550–1750* (Cambridge: Cambridge University Press,
1986), p. 147.

30. Stephen Orgel, *The Illusion of Power* (Berkeley: University of California Press, 1975), 40.

31. On the other hand, the instability of Hudibras as spectator and as a
spectacle brings the anti-masquerade of the poem into line with Stallybrass
and White's description of the popular fair in which the Other and the Same,
spectacle and spectator are "constantly renegotiated and unstable." See Peter
Stallybrass and Allon White, *The Politics and Poetics of Transgression* (London:
Methuen, 1986), 42.

32. Agnew, *Worlds Apart,* 103; Stephen Orgel, *The Jonsonian Masque*
Cambridge: Harvard University Press, 1965), 7.

33. Further evidence of this possibility occurs in Butler's early ballad
on the mock-coronation of Cromwell (quoted above, p. 7), in which the
protector's wife is celebrated as "Queen of a May-pole" and his daughter as
"Mayd-Marrian."

34. Wilders, introduction to *Hudibras,* xlvi.

35. Horne, "Butler's Use of the Rump in *Hudibras,*" 134; Seidel, *Satiric
Inheritance,* 113.

36. Korshin, *Typologies in England,* 281.

37. Wilders, commentary to *Hudibras* (440–41), quotes from John Eve-
lyn's *Diary* a description of the carnival horse races held in the Roman Corso.

38. *Satires,* 40.

*Chapter Five*

1. de Quehen, *Prose Observations,* xxiv. The *London Magazine* discovery
was made by Josephine Bauer in "Some Verse Fragments and Prose *Characters*
by Samuel Butler not Included in the *Complete Works.*" "War" and "A Covetous
Man" appear as "unclassified notes" in A. R. Waller's edition of *Characters and
Passages from Note-Books* (Cambridge: Cambridge University Press, 1908), pp.
472–74, 479–80. References to Butler's Characters in this chapter, cited
parenthetically by page number, are to Charles W. Daves's edition.

2. Waller (481) reprints Thyer's preface to Butler's Characters in the
*Genuine Remains.*

3. Benjamin Boyce, *The Polemic Character, 1640–1661* (Lincoln: University of Nebraska Press, 1955), 8. See also David Nichol Smith, *Characters*

*from the Histories & Memoirs of the Seventeenth Century* (Oxford: Clarendon Press, 1928), xxix–xxx.

4. Smith, ibid.

5. Daves, 17. I am indebted to Daves for the analogues in Earle and Cleveland mentioned in this paragraph.

6. W. J. Paylor, *The Overburian Characters* (Oxford: Oxford University Press, 1936), vii.

7. Jack, *Augustan Satire,* 31.

8. Wilders, introduction to *Hudibras,* xxii; de Quehen, *Prose Observations,* xxix.

9. Miner, *Restoration Mode,* 183.

10. Bentley, "Hudibras Butler," 86.

11. Nevo, *Dial of Virtue,* 233.

*Chapter Six*

1. Quoted by Bond, *English Burlesque Poetry,* 34.

2. *The Poems of John Cleveland,* ed. Brian Morris and Eleanor Withington (Oxford: Clarendon Press, 1967), 180.

3. Bond, *English Burlesque Poetry,* 263.

4. Ibid., 265.

5. Ibid., 319.

6. Included in *Poems on Affairs of State,* ed. Galbraith M. Crump, vol. 5 (New Haven: Yale University Press, 1968), 330–33.

7. Richards, *Hudibras in the Burlesque Tradition,* 41.

8. I rely upon Richards for this and for the titles cited later in this paragraph.

9. Elizabeth Cook, *Literary Influences in Colonial Newspapers* (New York: Columbia University Press, 1912), 134.

10. Bruce Ingham Granger, "Hudibras in the American Revolution," *American Literature,* 27 (1956):499–508.

11. Quoted by Granger, "Hudibras in the American Revolution," 507.

12. *The Satiric Poems of John Trumbull,* ed. Edwin T. Bowden (Austin: University of Texas Press, 1962), 103.

13. Richards, *Hudibras in the Burlesque Tradition,* 111.

14. Miner, *Restoration Mode,* 159, 196.

15. Ibid., 183.

16. David M. Vieth, "Rochester and the Restoration: An Introductory Note and Bibliography," *Papers in Language and Literature* 12 (1976): 263–64. See also Vieth's "Divided Consciousness: The Trauma and Triumph of Restoration Culture," *Tennessee Studies in Literature* 22 (1977): 46–62, and his introduction to *The Complete Poems of John Wilmot, Earl of Rochester* (New Haven: Yale University Press, 1968), xxxiii–xlii.

17. Margaret Anne Doody, *The Daring Muse: Augustan Poetry Reconsidered* (Cambridge: Cambridge University Press, 1985), 120–21.

# Selected Bibliography

PRIMARY SOURCES

*Collections*

*The Poetical Works of Samuel Butler.* 2 vols. Boston: Little, Brown, and Co., 1853. Contains memoir of Butler by Rev. John Mitford, *Hudibras,* and the poems in the *Genuine Remains.* Reissued in one volume by Houghton, Mifflin, n.d.

*The Poetical Works of Samuel Butler.* Introduction and notes by Rev. George Gilfillan. 2 vols. New York: D. Appleton and Co., 1854. Contains *Hudibras,* poems in the *Genuine Remains,* and "Various Readings and Additions to *Hudibras."*

*Hudibras Parts I and II and Selected Other Writings.* Edited by John Wilders and Hugh de Quehen. Oxford: Clarendon Press, 1973. Includes "The Elephant in the Moon," "Satire upon the Royal Society," several Characters, and passages from the notebooks. Fully annotated with bibliography. The only available paperback of Butler.

*Editions of* Hudibras

*Hudibras by Samuel Butler.* Memoir and notes by Treadway Russell Nash. London: T. Rickaby, 1793.

*Hudibras, by Samuel Butler.* Life, preface, and annotations by Zachary Grey. 3 vols. London: Charles and Henry Baldwyn, 1819. Contains selections from translations of *Hudibras,* plates, and useful index.

*Hudibras, by Samuel Butler.* Edited with an introduction by Henry G. Bohn. London: Bell and Sons, 1882. Contains notes by Grey and Nash, woodcuts by Thurston, and an index. Reissued 1907.

*Hudibras.* Edited by A. R. Waller. Cambridge: Cambridge University Press, 1905. Wanting editorial commentary, this edition has been supplanted by Wilders's.

*Hudibras.* Edited with an introduction and commentary by John Wilders. Oxford: Clarendon Press, 1967. Contains Butler's letter to George Oxenden and an index. The standard text of the poem.

*Other Works*


*Characters and Passages from Note-Books.* Edited by A. R. Waller. Cambridge: Cambridge University Press, 1908. Now supplanted by Daves's edition of the Characters and de Quehen's edition of the *Prose Observations*.

*Samuel Butler: Satires and Miscellaneous Poetry and Prose.* Edited by René Lamar. Cambridge: Cambridge University Press, 1928. The most complete edition of Butler's miscellaneous verse. Reprints the prose satires in Thyer's *Genuine Remains*.

*Samuel Butler: Three Poems.* Selected with an introduction by Alexander C. Spence. Augustan Reprint Society Publication no. 88. Los Angeles: Clark Memorial Library, 1961. Includes facsimilies of "To the Memory of . . . Du-Vall" (1671), and Thyer's printings of "Satyr on Our Ridiculous Imitation of the French," and the octosyllabic version of "The Elephant in the Moon."

*Samuel Butler 1612–1680: Characters.* Edited by Charles W. Daves. Cleveland: Press of Case Western Reserve Universities, 1970. Standard edition of 196 Characters, annotated. Includes a useful introduction.

*Samuel Butler: Prose Observations.* Edited with an introduction and commentary by Hugh De Quehen. Oxford: Clarendon Press, 1979. Standard edition of the prose manuscript materials (including William Longueville's Commonplace Book). Supplies a valuable index of topics.


## SECONDARY SOURCES


Anderson, P. B. "Anonymous Critic of Milton: Richard Leigh? or Butler?" *Studies in Philology* 44 (1947):504–18. Argues for Butler's authorship of *The Character of the Rump, The Censure of the Rota Upon Mr. Milton's Book . . . ,* and *The Transproser Rehears'd.*

Aubrey, John. *Brief Lives.* Edited by Andrew Clark. 2 vols. Oxford: Clarendon Press, 1898. Biographical notes by one of Butler's acquaintances.

Bauer, Josephine. "Some Verse Fragments and Prose *Characters* by Samuel Butler Not Included in the Complete Works." *Modern Philology* 45 (1948):160–68. Pieces together the verse fragments of Butler's comic narrative on medicine.

Bentley, Norma E. "Hudibras Butler." Ph.D. diss., Syracuse University, 1944. Primarily a study of Butler's thought, but also contains biographical and critical material.

————. " 'Hudibras' Butler Abroad." *Modern Language Notes* 40 (1945):254–59. Presents evidence of Butler's trip to France in 1670.

Bond, Richmond P. *English Burlesque Poetry: 1700–1750.* Cambridge: Harvard University Press, 1932. Defines the "Hudibrastic" form in English burlesque poetry. Includes a "Register of Burlesque Poems" published from 1700 to 1750.

Boyce, Benjamin. *The Polemic Character: 1640–1661.* Lincoln: University of Nebraska Press, 1955. The "Postscript: From Polemic Character to Verse Satire: *Hudibras,* Part I" traces the relationship between Butler's poem and the satiric rhetoric of the later prose Characters.

Bruun, Sv. "The Date of Samuel Butler's *The Elephant in the Moon,*" *English Studies* 55 (1974):133–39. Dates the poem between early August 1676 and November 1675.

———. "Who's Who in Samuel Butler's *The Elephant in the Moon,*" *English Studies* 50 (1969):381–89. Opposes Nicolson's identification of personages in Butler's satire on the Royal Society.

Cope, Kevin L. "The Conquest of Truth: Wycherly, Rochester, Butler, and Dryden and the Restoration Critique of Satire," *Restoration* 10 (1986):19–40. Restoration satire allows a "freedom to constitute ethical value according to any pleasing pattern—*so long as they* [the satirists] *remain superior to those patterns.*"

———. "The Infinite Perimeter: Human Nature and Ethical Mediation in Six Restoration Writers." *Restoration* 5 (1981):58–75. Permissible knowledge, for Butler, is so limited that it denies man's access to nature and heaven.

Cousins, A. D. "The Idea of a 'Restoration' and the Verse Satires of Butler and Marvell." *Southern Review* 14 (1981):131–42. Argues that for Butler the Restoration never occurred.

Craig, Hardin. "*Hudibras,* Part I, and the Politics of 1647." In *The Manly Anniversary Studies in Language and Literature,* 145–55. Chicago: University of Chicago Press, 1923. Dates the composition of part 1 of the poem using internal evidence.

Cunningham, Peter. "The Author of Hudibras at Ludlow Castle." *Notes and Queries* 1st ser., 5 (1852):5–6. Reprints evidence of Butler's employment as steward for Richard Vaughn.

Curtiss, Joseph T. "Butler's *Sidrophel.*" *PMLA* 44 (1929):1066–78. Discusses the development of Sidrophel as a satirical portrait. Butler's early ridicule of the astrologer William Lilly was made to accommodate the Royal Society member, Sir Paul Neile.

Davies, Paul C. "*Hudibras* and the 'proper Sphere of Wit.' " *Trivium* 5 (1970):104–15. Uses Butler's definition of "wit" as a point of departure for critical consideration of *Hudibras.*

De Beer, E. S. "The Later Life of Samuel Butler," *Review of English Studies* 4 (1928):159–66. Documents events of Butler's career and provides dates for the publication of *Hudibras* and the minor writings.

De Quehen, A. H. "An Account of Works Attributed to Samuel Butler." *Review of English Studies* 33 (1982):262–77. Estimates the authenticity of over eighty works in verse and prose attributed to Butler since 1680.

———. "Editing Butler's Manuscripts." In *Editing Seventeenth-Century Prose,* edited by D. I. B. Smith, 71–93. Toronto: Hakkert, 1972. Brilliant exercise in textual criticism of Butler's manuscript prose.

Donovan, J. "The 'Key to Hudibras' and Cleveland's 'The Character of a London Diurnall.' " *Notes and Queries* 20 (1973):175–76. Points out that the description of Isaac Robinson (Ralpho) in the "Key" was taken from a "fanciful creation" of Cleveland's.

Duffett, G. W. "The Name 'Hudibras.' " *Notes and Queries* 9 (1935):96. Finds a source for Hudibras's name in Jonson's *The New Inn.*

Edwards, Thomas R. "The Hero Emasculated: *Hudibras* and Mock-Epic." In *Imagination and Power: A Study of Poetry on Public Themes,* 39–44. New York: Oxford University Press, 1971. Argues that the satire of Hudibras is less political than sexual, the "gelding of heroic potency."

Engler, Balz. "*Hudibras* and the Problem of Satirical Distance." *English Studies* 60 (1979):436–43. Argues that the planes of reality and representation in the poem are too close to one another.

Farley-Hills, David. "Hudibras." In *Benevolence of Laughter: Comic Poetry of the Commonwealth and Restoration,* 46–71. Totowa: Rowman & Littlefield, 1974. Opposes the view of Butler as pessimist and skeptic, pointing out an unnoticed human and benevolent comedy in his writing.

———. *Rochester's Poetry,* 89–92, 101–104. London: Bell and Hyman, 1978. Defines burlesque as destruction "for the fun of destruction"; *Hudibras* is burlesque rather than satire.

Gibson, Dan, Jr. "Samuel Butler." In *Seventeenth Century Studies by Members of the Graduate School, University of Cincinnati,* edited by Robert Shafer, 277–335. Princeton: Princeton University Press, 1933. Reviews Butler's thinking on religion, science, and poetry.

Granger, Bruce Ingham. "Hudibras in the American Revolution." *American Literature* 27 (1956):499–508. Surveys the influence of *Hudibras* on eighteenth-century American verse.

Hill, Christopher. *The Collected Essays of Christopher Hill.* Vol. 1, *Writing and Revolution in Seventeenth Century England.* Amherst: University of Massachusetts Press, 1985. Treats Butler as a "radical royalist."

Horne, William C. " 'Between th' Petticoat and Breeches': Sexual Warfare and the Marriage Debate in *Hudibras.*" In vol. 11, *Studies in Eighteenth Century Culture,* edited by Harry C. Payne, 133–46. Madison: University of Wisconsin Press, 1982. Explains the marriage debate between Hudibras and the widow in terms of the seventeenth-century shift in the conception of marriage from a patriarchal to a contractual mode.

———. "Butler's Use of the *Rump* in *Hudibras.*" *Library Chronicle* 37

(1971):126–35. Argues that Butler's hero develops from a stock figure of ridicule found in *Rump*, a royalist anthology of satirical verse.

————. "Curiosity and Ridicule in Samuel Butler's Satire on Science." *Restoration* 7 (1983):8–18. Argues that Butler supported the Baconian movement, turning his satiric attacks not upon science generally, but upon particular scientists.

————. "Hard Words in *Hudibras*." *Durham University Journal* 75 (1983): 31–43. Considers *Hudibras* as a criticism and model of language abuse, "hard words" covering quarrels, religious cant, pedantic jargon, and harsh sounding language.

Jack, Ian. "Low Satire: *Hudibras*." In *Augustan Satire: Intention and Idiom in English Poetry: 1600–1750*, 15–42. Oxford: Clarendon Press, 1954. A general study of Butler's satire arguing that *Hudibras* is the opposite of the mock-heroic.

Korshin, Paul J. *Typologies in England: 1650–1820*, 277–82. Princeton: Princeton University Press, 1982. Investigates Butler's satire of the Renaissance tradition of mythography in *Hudibras*.

Lamar, René. "Du nouveau sur l'auteur d'*Hudibras:* Samuel Butler en Worcestershire." *Revue Anglo-Américaine* 1 (1924):213–27. A valuable source of information on Butler's ancestry and early life.

————. "Samuel Butler a l'École du Roi." *Études anglaises* 5 (1952): 17–24. Cautious speculation in the obscure area of Butler's early life.

————. "Samuel Butler et la Justice de son Temps." *Études anglaises* 7 (1954):271–79. Considers Butler's attitude toward law and the legal profession.

Laprevotte, Guy. " 'The Elephant in the Moon' de Samuel Butler: Le context et la satire." *Études anglaises* 25 (1972):465–78. Locates the context of Butler's satire in the controversy between Joseph Glanville and Henry Stubbe.

Leyburn, Ellen Douglass. "*Hudibras* Considered as Satiric Allegory." *Huntington Library Quarterly* 16 (1953):141–60. Reprinted in *Satiric Allegory: Mirror of Man*, 37–52. New Haven: Yale University Press, 1956. Reads *Hudibras* as an allegory not of particular persons or events, but of general human faults illustrated by the Puritans.

Miller, Ward S. "The Allegory in Part I of *Hudibras*." *Huntington Library Quarterly* 21 (1958):323–43. Interesting, but perhaps overingenious interpretation of *Hudibras* as both anti-Puritan and anti-Royalist satire.

Miner, Earl, "Butler: Hating Our Physician." In *The Restoration Mode from Milton to Dryden*, 158–97. Princeton: Princeton University Press, 1974. Judges *Hudibras* to be "a terrible, terrible great poem." An essential study of Butler.

Nelson, Nicolas H. "Astrology, *Hudibras*, and the Puritans." *Journal of the History of Ideas* 37 (1976):521–36. Argues that the seventeenth-century

debate between judicial astrologers and their Presbyterian critics underlies the debate between Sidrophel and Hudibras.

Nevo, Ruth. *The Dial of Virtue: A Study of Poems on Affairs of State in the
Seventeenth Century,* 189–204, 221–40. Princeton: Princeton University
Press, 1963. Assigns Butler an important place in the development of
seventeenth-century raillery.

Nicolson, Marjorie Hope. *Pepys' "Diary" and the New Science,* 122–57. Charlottesville: University Press of Virginia, 1965. Sheds considerable light
on the personages and events behind Butler's satires on science and the
Royal Society.

Nussbaum, Felicity A. "The Better Woman: The Amazon Myth and *Hudibras,"* 43–56. In *The Brink of All We Hate: English Satires on Women,
1660–1750,* Lexington: University of Kentucky, 1984. Argues that,
although sex roles and sexual ambiguities are central to the poem, *Hudibras* does not make a feminist statement.

Quintana, Ricardo. "Samuel Butler: A Restoration Figure in a Modern Light."
*English Literary History* 18 (1951):7–31. Surveys Butler's place, as both
satirist and moralist, in the history of Augustan literature. The first
major modern study of the satirist; still an important one.

———. "The Butler-Oxenden Correspondence." *Modern Language Notes* 48
(1933):1–11. Primary evidence concerning the composition of *Hudibras.*
The most important discovery in modern Butler scholarship.

Richards, Edward Ames. *Hudibras in the Burlesque Tradition.* Columbia University Studies in English and Comparative Literature, no. 127. New York:
Columbia University Press, 1937. Surveys the imitations of *Hudibras* in
England, Scotland, and America. Chapter 1, on Butler's personality,
may be the most perceptive treatment the poet has received. Contains a
valuable bibliography of "hudibrastic verse" to 1830.

Robinson, Ken. "The Skepticism of Butler's Satire on Science: Optimistic or
Pessimistic?" *Restoration* 7 (1983):1–7. Argues that Butler subscribed to
an optimistic epistemology and that "The Elephant in the Moon" is an
attack only on bad scientific method.

Seidel, Michael A. "Patterns of Anarchy and Oppression in Samuel Butler's
*Hudibras.*" *Eighteenth-Century Studies* 5 (1971):294–314. Adduces Butler's theory of satire ("controlled madness") and illustrates its application
to *Hudibras.*

———. "The Internecine Romance: Butler's *Hudibras.*" In *Satiric Inheritance:
Rabelais to Sterne,* 95–134. Princeton: Princeton University Press, 1979.
Interprets *Hudibras* as a violation of narrative generation or inheritance,
the romantic rituals of *Don Quixote* and *The Faerie Queene* becoming settle-
ments of war in *Hudibras.*

Snider, Alvin. "Babel Reversed: Samuel Butler's *Hudibras* and the Language of
Things." Ph.D. diss., University of Chicago, 1984. Interprets *Hudibras*

as a "language satire" that alerts the reader to "the ruins of Babel" and exploits the misuse of language to produce an "anti-style."

Staves, Susan. *Players' Scepters: Fictions of Authority in the Restoration*, 207–20. Lincoln: University of Nebraska Press, 1979. Objects to the general, philosophical reading of *Hudibras,* arguing instead that the poem is topical and doctrinaire.

Sutherland, W. O. S., Jr. *The Art of the Satirist: Essays on the Satire of Augustan England.* Austin: University of Texas Press, 1965. 54–71. Interesting chapter on *Hudibras* as a general satire on human nature.

Thorson, James L. "The Publication of *Hudibras.*" *Papers of the Bibliographical Society of America* 60 (1966):418–38. Bibliographical study of the three parts of *Hudibras.*

———. "Samuel Butler (1612–1680): A Bibliography." *Bulletin of Bibliography* 30 (1973):34–39. Covers biographical, bibliographical, and critical studies of Butler up to 1970. Includes a list of editions of note.

Totten, Charles F. "Hypocrisy and Corruption in Four Characters of Samuel Butler." *Essays in Literature* 2 (1974):164–70. Analyzes Butler's four longest Characters to reveal a theme of spreading corruption in society, religion, the arts, and science.

Troost, Linda V. "Poetry, Politics, and Puddings: The Imagery of Food in Butler's *Hudibras.*" *Restoration* 9 (1985):83–92. Argues that Butler equates food and Puritan politics as a satiric technique in *Hudibras.*

Veldkamp, Jan. *Samuel Butler, The Author of Hudibras.* Hilversum: De Atlas, 1923. Dated, but still useful for its treatment of the religious background of the poem and of Butler's relationship to Cervantes and Rabelais.

Vieth, David M. "Divided Consciousness: the Trauma and Triumph of Restoration Culture." *Tennessee Studies in Literature* 22 (1977):46–62. Describes *Hudibras* as a structure of "reversible meaning," one of four literary responses to the cultural revolution of the mid-seventeenth century.

Wasserman, George R. "A Strange Chimaera of Beasts and Men." *Studies in English Literature* 13 (1973):405–21. Investigates the argument and imagery of part 1 of *Hudibras.*

———. "Carnival in *Hudibras.*" *English Literary History* 55 (1988):79–97. Traces Butler's conception of hypocrisy as "Spiritual Carnival" in three parts of *Hudibras.*

———. "*Hudibras* and Male Chauvinism." *Studies in English Literature* 16 (1976):351–61. In parts 2 and 3 of *Hudibras,* Butler satirizes mankind by elevating women over men.

———. *Samuel Butler and the Earl of Rochester: A Reference Guide.* Boston: G. K. Hall, 1986. Lists and annotates studies of Butler up to 1984.

———. "Samuel Butler and the Problem of Unnatural Man." *Modern Language Quarterly* 31 (1970):179–94. Argues that Butler considered man both unnatural and irrational.

Wilding, Michael. "Butler and Gray's Inn." *Notes and Queries* 216 (1971): 293–95. Presents evidence of Butler's legal background.

————. "Samuel Butler at Barbourne." *Notes and Queries* 13 (1966): 15–19. Biographical information on Butler's early school days.

————. "The Date of Samuel Butler's Baptism." *Review of English Studies* 17 (1966):174–77. New information on the Butler family.

————. "The Last of the Epics: The Rejection of the Heroic in *Paradise Lost* and *Hudibras*." In *Restoration Literature: Critical Approaches,* edited by Harold Love, 91–120. London: Methuen & Co., 1972. Compares *Hudibras* and *Paradise Lost* as reactions against the heroic tradition provoked by the realities of civil war.

Wood, Anthony à. *Athenae Oxonienses.* Edited by Philip Bliss. Vol 3. London: F. C. & J. Rivington, 1813–20. Includes available biographical information on Butler in the article on William Prynne.

# Index

Addison, Joseph, 62
Agnew, Jean-Christophe, 109
"Alphabetical Key to Hudibras," 50–51
Anderson, Paul Bunyan, 142n27
Aristotle, 29, 36, 37, 79, 82, 122, 126
Aubrey, John, 1, 3, 4, 5, 10, 16

Bacon, Francis, 2, 19, 30, 126
Bagehot, Walter, 61
Bakhtin, Mikhail, 48, 63, 100, 101, 102, 103, 104, 105, 106, 108
Bauer, Josephine, 20
Beaumont, Francis, 47
Benlowes, Edward, 114, 127
Bentley, Norma, 45, 129, 141n5, 145n21, 146n17
Boas, George, 74, 78
Boileau, Nicolas, 13, 14, 73
Bond, Richmond P., 58–59, 131
Boyce, Benjamin, 113
Boyle, Robert, 32
Brereton, Sir William, 9
Brooks, Harold, 13
Brunn, Sv., 143n48, 145n8
Buckingham, Duke of. See Villiers
Burnet, Gilbert, 69
Burton, Robert, 75
Butler, Samuel (1613–80):
    birth, 1; education, 2; early employment, 2–3; early writings, 6–8; relations with court wits, 11–12, 14–15; last years and death, 16–17; methods of composition, 19–20; methods of satire, 7, 38–41; views on astrology, 68; on folly, 22, 27–28, 76, 79, 118; on hypocrisy, 26, 57–58, 100–12; on ignorance, 23, 27, 28–29, 40, 55–57, 64, 76, 79, 80, 82; on imagination and fancy, 28, 34, 36, 39; on nature, 22, 24, 28–29; on poetry, epic and romance, 33–41, 54; on poli-

tics, 36, 41–44; on reason, 22–24, 27–28, 31, 32, 33, 36, 37–38, 45, 75–77, 79, 80, 82, 83, 98; on religion, 32, 41, 42, 44–45; on sicnece, 14, 29–33, 74; on the senses, 23, 28–30, 37, 80; on truth, 22, 25, 33, 34, 35, 36, 38, 80; on wit, 26, 28, 34–36, 38–39, 54, 62

WRITINGS: PROSE

*Case of King Charles I, The (The Plagiary Exposed)*, 6, 17, 135
Characters, 2, 4, 5, 10, 12, 15, 16, 18, 19, 25, 27, 28, 29, 34, 35, 36–37, 38, 40, 42, 43, 54, 55, 76, 77, 113–29, 130, 139, 142n25
*Lord Roos His Answer to the Marquesse of Dorchester's Letter*, 7, 18
*Mola Asinaria*, 7, 17, 18
"Occasional Reflection on Dr. Charlton's Feeling a Dog's Pulse at Gresham-College, An," 14, 74
Prose Observations, 2, 10, 12–13, 14, 15, 16, 18, 19, 24–37, 39–40, 41–45, 50, 54, 55–56, 57, 58, 68, 74, 75–76, 81–82, 93, 100, 108, 113, 117, 118, 122, 130, 138, 139, 143n47
*Speech Made at the Rota, A,* 6, 7
*Two Letters, One from John Audland . . . The Other, William Prynne's Answer*, 17
*Two Speeches Made in the Rump Parliament,* 6

WRITINGS: VERSE

"Ballad, A," 8, 52, 150n33
"Cydippe, Her Answer to Acontius," 16
"Elephant in the Moon, The," 14, 15, 29–33, 35, 54, 143n46